FOREVER PARIS

Library of Congress Cataloging-in-Publication Data

Henry de Tessan, Christina

Forever Paris : 25 walks in the footsteps of Chanel, Hemingway, Picasso, and more /
Christina Henry de Tessan.

p. cm.

ISBN 978-1-4521-0488-1 (hardcover)

1. Paris (France)—Guidebooks. 2. Walking—France—Paris—Guidebooks.
I. Title.

DC708.D49 2012

914.4'361048412—dc23

2011016489

Manufactured in China.

Designed by Suzanne LaGasa.
Typesetting by Happenstance Type-O-Rama.

10 9 8 7 6 5 4

Chronicle Books LLC
680 Second Street
San Francisco, California 94107
www.chroniclebooks.com

FSC
www.fsc.org

MIX
Paper from
responsible sources
FSC® C016973

PHOTO CREDITS. Cover image: courtesy of Tasha Winton (www.tashawinton.co.uk); **p. 9:** © 2011 Estate of Pablo Picasso/
Artists Rights Society (ARS), New York; Réunion des Musées Nationaux / Art Resource, NY; **p. 13:** Library of Congress,
Prints & Photographs Division, Miscellaneous Items in High Demand Collection. LC-USZ62-102576; **p. 17:** Ernest Hemingway
outside of his residence at 113 rue Notre-Dame-des-Champs, Paris, c. 1924. Photograph in the Ernest Hemingway Photograph
Collection/John F. Kennedy Presidential Library and Museum, Boston; **p. 21:** Library of Congress, Prints & Photographs
Division, Miscellaneous Items in High Demand Collection. LC-USZ62-111592; **p. 25:** Office of War Information, Overseas
Picture Division; **p. 29:** Title page of *Old Goriot*, 1834; **p. 33:** Photo by Stanislaus Walery, 1926, via Wikimedia Commons;
p. 37: Photographer unknown, c. 1930s, via Wikimedia Commons; **p. 41:** *Moulin de la Galette*, 1889, Henri de Toulouse-Lautrec,
via Wikimedia Commons; **p. 45:** Photo by Paul Child. The Schlesinger Library, Radcliffe Institute, Harvard University; **p. 49:**
Photo by Gaspard-Félix Tournachon, date unknown, via Wikimedia Commons; **p. 53:** Photo by Gertrude Käsebier, 1905, via
Wikimedia Commons; **p. 57:** Frontispiece of an 1840 edition of *Théâtre français—Œuvres de Molière*, Éditeurs Martial Ardant
frères; photograph by Jodelet/Lépinay; **p. 61:** Dmitri Kessel/Time&Life Pictures/Getty Images; **p. 65:** *Portrait of Napoléon in
his Study at the Tuileries*, Jacques-Louis David, 1812, via Wikimedia Commons; **p. 69:** Photo by Gaspard-Félix Tournachon,
1865, via Wikimedia Commons; **p. 73:** Bentley Archive/Popperfoto/Getty Images; **p. 77:** Cover of *Jours de France*, February 17,
1955. From *Audrey Hepburn: International Cover Girl*, by Scott Brizel; **p. 81:** Photo by Gaspard-Félix Tournachon, c. 1870, via
Wikimedia Commons; **p. 85:** *Portrait af Marie Antoinette at Age 12*, Martin van Meytens, 1767, via Wikimedia Commons;
p. 89: left: Library of Congress, Prints & Photographs Division, Van Vechten Collection. LC-USZ62-42523, 1959; right: Library
of Congress, Prints & Photographs Division, NYWT&S Collection, reproduction number LC-USZ62- 112039, 1940; **p. 93:** *Rue
Montorgueil, Paris, Festival af June 30, 1878*, 1878, Claude Monet, via Wikimedia Commons; **p. 97:** Jean-Jacques Bernier/
Gamma-Rapho/Getty Images; **p. 101:** Photo by Carl Van Vechten, 1933, via Wikimedia Commons; **105:** Photographer unknown,
date unknown, Collection Centre d'études Colette.

FOREVER PARIS

25 WALKS IN THE FOOTSTEPS OF CHANEL, HEMINGWAY, PICASSO, AND MORE

Christina Henry de Tessan

CHRONICLE BOOKS
SAN FRANCISCO

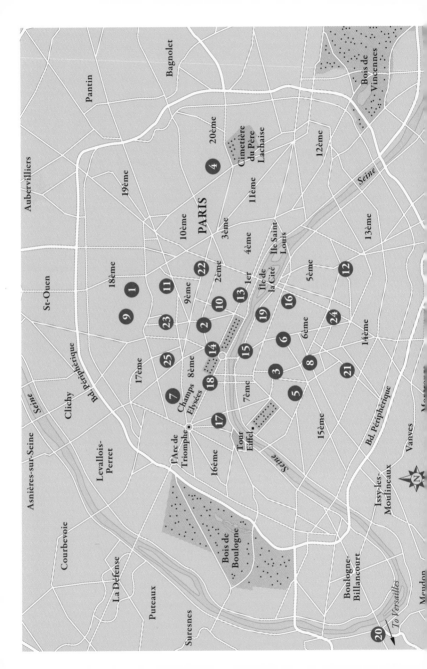

CONTENTS

INTRODUCTION

I love Paris. And I know I'm not alone in that regard. I've strategized long and hard to find ways to spend time there on a regular basis. I love visiting favorite places that I know will deliver a happy *frisson* of delight when I step inside—the paper shop where I once bought my wedding invitations, whose fragile old door still signals my arrival with that familiar little jingle; my favorite, intimate, packed-to-the-rafters bookshop; the Luxembourg Gardens on a crisp autumn day; the satisfaction of knowing where to buy the best *chausson aux pommes*. And the list goes on. But I also love Paris because it never fails to teach me something new. No matter how many times I've walked its streets, I always happen upon some detail that I've never noticed before—a plaque identifying where someone lived, a centuries-old restaurant hidden down some side street, a specialty museum I never knew existed, a new *patissier*, even a graceful new bridge arcing across the Seine. Each discovery offers me a fresh chance to fall in love with the city anew.

This guide follows in the footsteps of twenty-seven of Paris's most famous artists, authors, lovers, politicians, and ne'er-do-wells. From Napoléon Bonaparte to Coco Chanel to Serge Gainsbourg, the intimate walking tours within illuminate the lives and loves of some of Paris's best-known devotees. But this guide also shows how important the city itself is to their stories, and what a catalyst it has been over time. Paris, in many cases, helped these people find their calling. They used the city as their muse, drew inspiration from its beauty, exposed its underbelly, and, in every single case, were transformed and elevated by it. As a result, they went on to change the course of art, fashion, food, philosophy, politics, and beyond. The well-loved streets are not just

atmospheric (though they are that) or full of pretty things (though they most definitely are that too). They have served as a force for change—compelling these people to create something new, whether it was the first little black dress or the first Modernist painting.

As for how to use this guide, it should be quite straightforward. For each person featured, you'll find a brief history that focuses on Paris's role in their life and an accompanying walk that leads you to the places that were important to them. Metro stops are indicated at the start of the walk, and destinations covered on the walk are highlighted in bold and numbered. The numbers correspond to the map and follow the walking route. Most of the walks take place in a single neighborhood, though a few require that you hop on the metro (these are marked). At the end of some walks, you'll find additional options for further "research" relevant to the walk. These might include places to go to hear jazz, restaurants to savor, or museums to explore. All walks begin and end at metro stops (with the exception of the Marie Antoinette walk).

As you retrace the steps of some of Paris's most illustrious residents—walking along both familiar boulevards and unknown streets, eating and drinking at their favorite spots, exploring their neighborhoods, seeing where they painted, wrote, argued, learned, loved, and lived—you can see the city with a fresh eye and come to appreciate its intoxicating, inspiring power as never before.

Pablo Picasso

"Without Paris . . . Picasso would not have been Picasso."
— Art critic John Russell

Pablo Picasso arrived in Paris from Spain in 1900 at the age of nineteen. He settled in Montmartre, a labyrinthine village on the northern edge of Paris. Although he shuttled back and forth between Barcelona and Paris for a few years, he made Paris his permanent home in 1904. Because it was cut off from the rest of the city, Montmartre had long drawn artists and bohemians in search of cheap accommodations. As a result, it had become a densely packed melting pot of young foreigners in search of creative inspiration and freedom from the constraints of their provincial hometowns.

Picasso was thrilled to escape the confines of his overly constricting native country, and dove headlong into the seductive Montmartre scene. He found a studio in a dilapidated building dubbed the "Bateau Lavoir," or the "Laundry Barge" (thus named because, with the laundry hanging from the windows, it resembled the laundry boats on the Seine). Although the studio was primitive (no gas, no electricity), Picasso was at last free to roll up his sleeves and pursue his passion in earnest. He started out by selling his artwork for a few *sous* on the streets, until the eminent Gertrude Stein became a devoted patron. She was crucial to his early success, supporting him financially and exposing his work to other buyers through her salons.

Parisian artists and intellectuals at the time were seeking to break with the past. In Paris, Picasso found not only support for his style, but also a community that challenged him, fueling his already formidable creative drive. He befriended avant-garde poets and painters, with whom he'd carouse late into the night, feverishly debating art and poetry. It was during this time that he and his friend Georges Braque hit upon Cubism, a watershed moment in the history of art.

World War I ushered in an era of change. As a foreign noncombatant, Picasso didn't join the war effort, but many of his friends did. His eclectic community dissolved overnight. In 1912, Picasso moved to Montparnasse, the new center of the artistic world. There, he mingled with a new group of artists, among them poet Jean Cocteau. Montparnasse was a hive of creativity. A building dubbed "La Ruche" (the beehive) was home to painters from across the globe— Chagall, Rivera, Zadkine, and more.

Modigliani, Man Ray, and Matisse all passed through the area at one point or another. The unprecedented density of artists in one neighborhood—even one building—was a crucial catalyst for the rapidly changing art scene. This cross-fertilization led to intensely fruitful collaborations, such as the 1917 Ballets Russes production of *Parade*, on which Picasso collaborated with Cocteau and composer Erik Satie. Paris had never seen anything like it, and Picasso's fame spread.

From that point on, Picasso made a stratospheric ascent through the artistic ranks, going on to become a pillar of the Modernist movement. He continued to paint prolifically for the rest of his life, delving into ceramics and sculpture as well. Continually encouraged to innovate and experiment, he pushed modern art to places it had never been before.

M: ABBESSES

Head west out of the square and turn right on rue Ravignan. Continue straight up the stairs to a small triangular plaza. You will see a restored version of the famous **Bateau Lavoir** (**1**; 13 rue Ravignan) on your left; a window displays old photographs of the building, as well as snapshots of Picasso and his friends. Once a piano manufacturing factory, the oddly shaped wooden building was converted to primitive artists' studios when Picasso arrived on the scene in 1904. Rickety and squalid, it had only one toilet for all the residents and only cold running water, but the studio was full of light and the social atmosphere was unlike anything he'd ever experienced. Picture it in its heyday: a young and anonymous Picasso and his poet friends stumbling back late at night to his studio, on which he'd chalked "Au Rendez-Vous des Poètes," debating art and philosophy as the sun rose. It is here that he painted the famous *Les Demoiselles d'Avignon*.

Now continue up the hill and veer right. Then take the first left, which will put you on rue des Saules. **Au Lapin Agile** (**2**; 22 rue des Saules) was one of the artist's favorite haunts. In those days, he had so little money that he often traded his paintings for food. Take a step back in time and come back later for drinks and a show (nightly at 9 P.M.). Backtrack and consider stopping at **La Bonne Franquette** (**3**; 2 rue des Saules), a long-standing artists' haunt frequented once upon a time by the likes of Picasso, Van Gogh, and Toulouse-Lautrec. Take the second left onto rue Norvins, then turn right on rue Poulbot. Loop around to the left, then head down the stairs at the end. Turn left down rue Gabrielle and take your first right on rue Drevet. Turn right on rue de la Vieuville, then left on rue des Martyrs and right on bd. de Clichy. When Picasso started making money, he decamped to **#11** (**4**) with his mistress. Although the relationship didn't last, this move from a squalid and dilapidated artist's studio to a light and airy apartment marked the beginning of a more prosperous phase in Picasso's life. Catch the metro at Pigalle.

To explore the artwork that made Picasso famous, visit the Musée Picasso (5 rue de Thorigny, 3rd), which holds some five thousand works, including the works Picasso was never willing to part with. A few blocks away, the Centre Pompidou houses one of the world's greatest collections of modern art; here you can see Picasso's work alongside that of the artists he influenced.

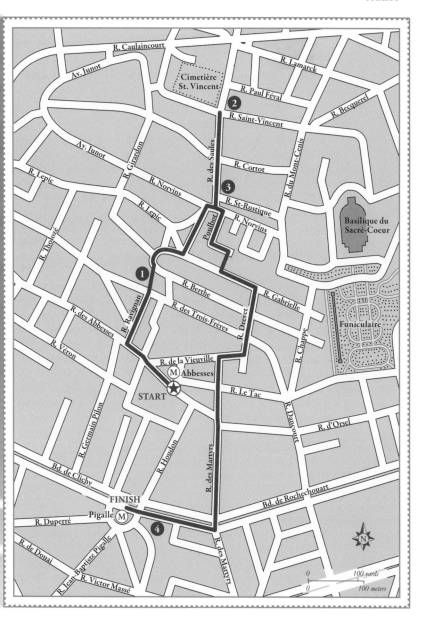

Coco Chanel

"Fashion is not something that exists in dresses only.
Fashion is in the sky, in the street, fashion has to do with ideas,
the way we live, what is happening."

Practically single-handedly, Coco Chanel revolutionized women's fashion—no small feat for an orphan raised in the French countryside. It is thanks largely to her unwavering confidence and intuitive understanding of the changing times that women are no longer trussed in corsets, hemmed in by petticoats, and pinned down by gargantuan hats.

Chanel's rags-to-riches story is the stuff of fantasy (literally in some cases, as Chanel often reinvented details about her past). Abandoned by her father at age twelve following her mother's death, a young Gabrielle Chanel (her real name) spent several years in a convent, where she learned to sew. With a combination of personal savvy and hard-headed brio, she became the mistress of a high-society horse breeder, who exposed her to the lifestyle of the upper classes.

She finally arrived in Paris in 1909, funded by another suitor, Boy Capel, who encouraged her—on a lark—to pursue a foray into the hat business. At the time, women were wearing elaborate concoctions that limited their range of movement and required the assistance of maids—both to help affix the hats properly with hat pins, and

then to remove them. In her typically clear-eyed way, Chanel concluded that this trend was utterly ridiculous and took it upon herself to set things straight. She bought some straw boaters from the Galeries Lafayette, and embellished each with a ribbon or flower. Done. They were liberating, elegant—and revolutionary. Parisians came flocking.

From hats, Chanel moved on to apparel, applying the same principles to her clothing designs. "Simplicity is the keynote of all true elegance," she quipped. Women were just then making strides toward greater independence, and many embraced her modern look. With the onset of World War I, simplicity in dress became appropriate, and Chanel's reputation flourished. She went from triumph to triumph, setting trends that continue to define fashion today. In 1921, she launched her perfume line with Chanel No. 5, one of the world's best-selling scents even today. In 1926, her famous little black dress transformed funereal black into the ultimate symbol of chic.

In Paris, Chanel was able to closely observe how women's lives were changing—and then conceive the kinds of

designs that would resonate with them. And only in Paris could she have found the necessary assortment of monied, trendsetting customers who could use their influence to change others' ideas about fashion. Although Paris was already an established center of fashion when Chanel appeared on the scene, she ensured that it remained that way for decades to come.

At the beginning of World War II, Chanel closed her business, stating firmly, "this is not a time for fashion." After the war, she was condemned for her affair with a German officer and retreated to Switzerland for several years. However, she made a triumphant comeback in 1954, thanks largely to the patronage of high-profile Americans such as Jackie Kennedy. From then on, the brand's name was assured. A tireless workaholic, Chanel worked until the day before she died, which she did at the Ritz in 1971.

M: Opéra

Head down bd. des Capucines and turn left on rue Cambon. Chanel opened her second hat shop, "Chanel Modes," at **21 rue Cambon** (**1**) in 1910 and expanded to shops in several buildings on the block. Today, you'll find her latest designs (created for many years by Karl Lagerfeld, another of the world's most celebrated designers). Chanel's personal apartment is located on the third floor (2e étage) of **31 rue Cambon** (**2**), and has been left exactly as it was when she died (sadly, it is not open to the public). It is a shrine to her personal taste: Chinese coromandel screens, the camellias that appear in her designs, shafts of wheat (a symbol of prosperity), and a chandelier that she designed with hidden references to herself (G for Gabrielle, 5 for Chanel No. 5). Although Chanel spent much of her life in this building, she didn't actually sleep here (in fact, her apartment didn't even have a bedroom). Across the street is the discreet back entrance to the **Ritz** (**3**), where she kept a suite for years, and this is where she retreated every evening at the end of her long workday. (For a pretty penny, you can book her suite.) Continue down the street and turn left on rue du Faubourg St-Honoré. As you stroll past the chic boutiques along here, consider the way Chanel's earliest musings on fashion more than one hundred years ago continue to influence the cutting-edge designs on display today. Chanel owned another apartment at **29 rue du Faubourg St-Honoré** (**4**), where she held a famous diamond jewelry exhibit in 1932. Always ahead of her time, Chanel designed a necklace that wrapped around the neck like a scarf and featured a star; the *collier comette* contained more than six hundred diamonds. Continue straight and turn right on rue de Castiglione. Turn left on rue de Rivoli, stopping at **Angelina** (**5**; 226 rue de Rivoli), a *salon de thé* frequented by Chanel (although known for her tireless work ethic, she did occasionally take time to relax here). Continue to the **Musée des Arts Décoratifs** (**6**). The fashion-related exhibits are always changing, but it's worth checking on the current show. Whether you happen upon a multi-designer exhibit or a single-designer retrospective, they are always illuminating. At the Place du Palais Royal, turn left to enter the Jardins du Palais Royal. The king of vintage wares, Didier Ludot, owns three boutiques beneath the picturesque arcades, including one whose name Chanel undoubtedly would have approved of: **La Petite Robe Noire** (or, The Little Black Dress) (**7**; 20–24 gal. Montpensier and 125 gal. Valois). Catch the metro at Palais Royal–Musée du Louvre.

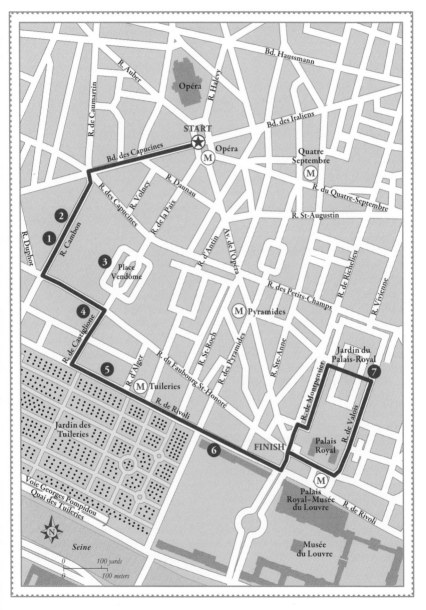

START

Opéra

Bd. Haussmann

R. Auber

Opéra

R. Halévy

Bd. des Italiens

Quatre Septembre

Bd. des Capucines

R. de Caumartin

R. Daunau

R. du Quatre-Septembre

R. des Capucines

R. Volney

R. de la Paix

R. St-Augustin

2

1

R. Cambon

R. Duphot

3

Place Vendôme

R. d'Antin

Av. de l'Opéra

R. des Petits-Champs

R. de Richelieu

R. Vivienne

4

R. de Castiglione

M Pyramides

R. St-Roch

R. des Pyramides

R. Ste-Anne

Jardin du Palais-Royal

7

5

R. d'Alger

R. du Faubourg St-Honoré

R. de Montpensier

R. de Valois

M Tuileries

R. de Rivoli

6

FINISH

Palais Royal

Jardin des Tuileries

Voie Georges Pompidou

Quai des Tuileries

M Palais Royal–Musée du Louvre

R. de Rivoli

N

Seine

Musée du Louvre

0 100 yards
0 100 meters

ERNEST HEMINGWAY

"If you are lucky enough to have lived in Paris as a young man, then wherever you go for the rest of your life, it stays with you, for Paris is a moveable feast."

"When spring came, even the false spring, there were no problems except where to be happiest," writes Ernest Hemingway in *A Moveable Feast*, in which he chronicles his life in Paris in detail. In fact, he himself writes in such glowing terms about his time there that one feels utterly transported to that time and place when reading his account.

Hemingway arrived in Paris in late 1921 at the age of twenty-two with his wife Hadley. He embraced the city with the same intensity that he did everything else in his life, and soon became the embodiment of 1920s expatriate Paris. The polar opposite of conservative, Prohibition-era America, post–World War I Paris proved an intoxicating elixir for Hemingway, liberating the young writer intellectually and embedding him in an eclectic and stimulating community of expat writers and artists. Suddenly, Hemingway seemed to be everywhere all the time: drinking with friends, teaching boxing, talking shop with other writers, carrying on illicit romances, walking the streets, and, oh yes, writing some of his greatest works in what little time he had left.

Reluctant to spend money in his early days in Paris, Hemingway took to wandering the streets for entertainment. Early on, he came upon the English-language bookstore Shakespeare & Company, where he met the owner, Sylvia Beach. He later said, "No one that I ever knew was nicer to me." In no time at all, Beach had taken him under her wing, loaning him money and expanding his intellectual horizons by loading him up with Dostoevsky, Turgenev, and D. H. Lawrence. It was at this bookstore that Hemingway first encountered Ezra Pound. He also met Gertrude Stein early on, and soon found himself strolling across the Luxembourg Gardens in the afternoons to visit her. Later, he was meeting up with pals F. Scott Fitzgerald, Ezra Pound, and James Joyce in the cafés of Montparnasse for what often turned into multiple rounds of drinks.

When he arrived in Paris, Hemingway was just an unknown correspondent for *The Toronto Star*. But with the support of mentors such as Joyce, Beach, Pound, and Stein, he doggedly pursued his own writing, toiling away daily at his favorite table at the Closerie des Lilas, which became a home away from home for him. His first novel, *The Sun Also Rises*,

depicting the Bohemian expat life in Paris and the running of the bulls in Pamplona, Spain, was published in 1926. And with that, he left obscurity behind forever.

Hemingway left Paris in 1928 with a new wife, Pauline, but he returned several times in the following years, most famously in 1944 to "liberate" the Ritz (and, more importantly, its wine cellar) after the Nazi occupation of Paris. Apparently, he hosted one of the most famous parties the Ritz has ever seen. According to legend, his friend photographer Robert Capa raced into Paris determined to make it to the Ritz before anyone else, only to find Hemingway already enjoying a drink at the bar—which is why it's called the Hemingway Bar today.

M: Cardinal Lemoine

Head up rue du Cardinal Lemoine to #74 (**1**), where Hemingway lived with his wife Hadley when they first arrived in Paris in 1922. They lived in a two-room apartment with a shared bathroom down the hall, but, he said later, "We were very poor and very happy." Continue to place de la Contrescarpe, depicted in the opening of *A Moveable Feast*. To the left is rue Mouffetard, which Hemingway describes as a "wonderful narrow crowded market street." Cross onto rue Blainville, then rue de l'Estrapade, which turns into rue des Fossés St-Jacques. Turn right on rue St-Jacques and left on rue Soufflot to enter the **Luxembourg Gardens** (**2**), where Hemingway strolled almost daily. Turn left at the fountain and head south out of the gardens on Av. de l'Observatoire to reach the ivy-shrouded **Closerie des Lilas** (**3**; 171 bd. du Montparnasse). Hemingway's favorite café (the quietest of the Montparnasse cafés), it's rumored to be the place where he wrote *The Sun Also Rises*. A plaque at the bar shows where he used to sit. Take rue Notre-Dame-des-Champs. Hemingway lived in a courtyard-facing apartment at #113 (**4**; unmarked). His friend Ezra Pound lived down the street; Pound supposedly traded Hemingway writing help for boxing lessons. Backtrack and head north, veer left on rue d'Assas, then turn left on rue de Fleurus. Gertrude Stein's apartment was at #27 (**5**). Hemingway spent many hours here (before they had a falling out), during which time they gossiped and talked about writing, surrounded by the paintings of Picasso and Matisse. Head into the Luxembourg Gardens. Exit onto rue Férou, turn right on rue St-Sulpice, then right on rue de l'Odéon, a route Hemingway choreographed to avoid the temptations of the neighborhood restaurants he could not afford. The original **Shakespeare & Company** (**6**; 12 rue de l'Odéon) was a beloved address of many writers, who used it as a lending library, a source of inspiration and moral support, and a networking hub. For Hemingway, it was nothing less than a spiritual home. Continue up the street and turn left on rue Racine to reach **Polidor** (**7**; 41 rue Monsieur le Prince), where Hemingway dined in his poorer days. Head up rue Monsieur le Prince and turn left on bd. St-Germain to reach **Brasserie Lipp** (**8**; 151 bd. St-Germain) and the **Deux Magots** (**9**; 6 pl. St-Germain-des-Prés), two of his favorite places. In *A Moveable Feast*, Hemingway describes a meal at Lipp, in which he consumed a very cold beer, potato salad, and *cervelas*, a sausage with mustard sauce. Consider paying tribute to the writer by doing the same. Catch the metro at St-Germain-des-Prés.

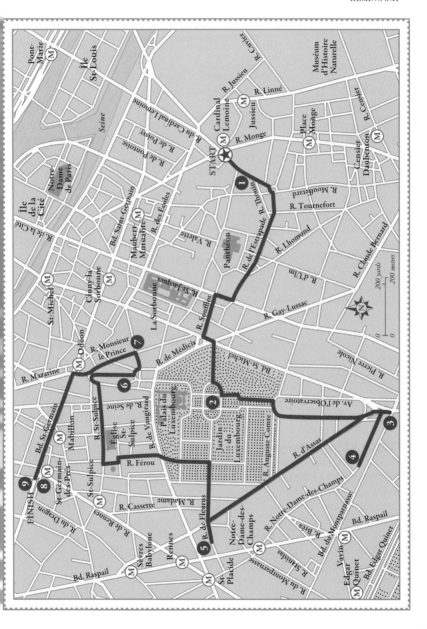

$\mathscr{E}$DITH $\mathscr{P}$IAF

"Paris, tu es ma gaieté, Paris."
("Paris, you are my joy, Paris.")

Few songs have the power to create the kind of piercing nostalgia that many of us feel when we hear Edith Piaf singing, "Non, je ne regrette rien." Wrung from the depths of her soul, sung with almost overpowering sincerity, the words perfectly capture the tension between despair and hope—an apt reflection of Piaf's extraordinary life.

Edith Piaf is as famous for her hardscrabble youth in Belleville, a rough neighborhood on the fringes of Paris, as she is for her songs. Legend has it that she was born in 1915 on the neighborhood's streets, but evidence indicates that she actually entered the world more conventionally, at a local hospital. She endured a highly unstable and semi-nomadic childhood, living for a while with her maternal grandparents, then moving to a brothel in Normandy run by her father's mother. Eventually, she began touring with her father, who performed on the streets throughout France, and at the age of fifteen she returned to Belleville, where she continued to sing on the streets and in neighborhood dance halls. Still a teenager, she fell in love and had a baby, but her child died young, and she moved on to new lovers.

Piaf had lived long and hard by the time she was "discovered" at the age of nineteen by a talent-spotter on a street corner near the Champs-Élysées. She was catapulted into the limelight and remained there for the rest of her life. Although she had fame, Piaf was plagued by personal tragedy, drug addiction, and health problems throughout her life. Through it all, despite her hardships, she continued to sing. It wasn't just her voice—which was certainly extraordinary—but also the outpouring of emotion in her songs that made her such a beloved figure. Her rags to riches story captured the imagination of the world, and she used her deeply personal understanding of life's challenges to seduce audiences everywhere.

It is difficult to imagine that Edith Piaf could have become who she was anywhere other than Paris. The city was an intrinsic part of her personal identity and public persona. In Paris, she found an audience that understood where she came from. People loved her for her *populaire* (common) background. The sharp contrast between her gritty youth and her glittering life as an international star was a crucial element of her songs. Although she eventually found success

around the world, Parisian audiences always understood her best, and she always returned to them.

Piaf's line, "Je repars à zéro" ("I'm starting over again"), couldn't be more appropriate. Despite countless setbacks, she pressed on, singing, "Je me fous du passé"—("I don't give a damn about the past"). The diminutive singer with the magnificent voice always looked ahead and rose again, enjoying greater success with each reincarnation. She chose to see *la vie en rose.*

M: Jourdain

Exit onto rue de Belleville. The church before you, **St-Jean Baptiste de Belleville (1)**, is where Piaf's father's funeral was held in 1944. Turn left (when you're facing the church) and head down rue de Belleville. This *quartier populaire* (working-class neighborhood) has served as a first stop for generations of immigrants from around the world. Piaf was indelibly shaped by this down-and-out area on the edge of the city, and nearly every mention of Belleville includes her name. Although she lived and worked in other parts of the city over the course of her life, she spent her formative years here and could often be found singing on these very street corners. Piaf was semi-nomadic for many years, renting rooms in hotels and apartments for short periods. One of those places is at **115 rue de Belleville (2)**, where she lived for a period with her father. At **#72 (3)** is a plaque showing the building where Piaf was supposedly born. According to legend, her mother gave birth to her right on the front stoop with the help of two policemen while her father went off to get help—stopping in bars along the way. (The facts are rather less colorful: Her birth certificate states that she was born at the nearby Hôpital Tenon.) Farther down the hill on the left is **Aux Folies (4**; 8 rue de Belleville), a tatty but atmospheric neighborhood bar that once operated as a *café-théâtre* where Piaf sang in her early days. Continue straight onto rue du Faubourg du Temple, where you'll find **La Java (5;** 105 rue du Faubourg du Temple), another concert hall that Piaf made famous. Backtrack and turn right on bd. de Belleville. (If you time your visit for a Tuesday or Friday, you'll see the action-packed open-air market in full swing down the meridian.) Turn right on rue Oberkampf and left on rue Crespin-du-Gast. Housed in a private residence at #5 is the **Musée Edith Piaf** (**6**; open 1 P.M. to 6 P.M.; you must call 01-43-55-52-72 in advance to make an appointment and get a code for entry). Piaf actually lived in this apartment when she was eighteen. This diminutive but fascinating shrine to the singer contains an impressive collection of personal items: letters of praise from celebrities around the world, one of her trademark black dresses, handbags, gloves, shoes, photos, and more. Piaf's music plays in the background. Backtrack to the boulevard and continue south to the Cimetière du Père Lachaise. You'll find a map at the entrance that shows exactly where **Piaf's grave (7)** is located (on the other side of the cemetery). Catch the metro back near the cemetery entrance.

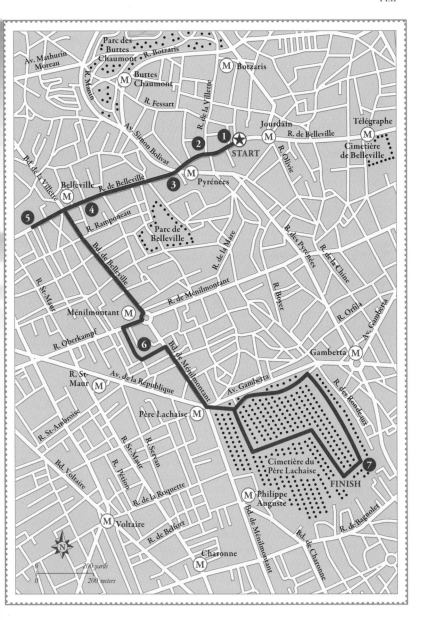

CHARLES DE GAULLE

"Never relinquish the initiative."

Simultaneously demonized and mythologized, Charles de Gaulle had an undeniably powerful influence on twentieth-century France. He became a dominant figure at the onset of World War II and rarely left the limelight until 1969. During those three decades, he represented the Free French during World War II, ensured that the country had a voice after the war, led two provisional governments, became president, inaugurated the Fifth Republic, granted Algeria independence, and steered the country through the 1968 riots. Like him or not, he left an indelible mark on modern-day France.

De Gaulle was born in 1890 in Lille. He entered the military and fought in World War I, where he was recognized for his valiant fighting. Afterward, he worked his way through the military ranks until the Germans invaded France in 1940.

This was his defining moment. Rather than surrender with the rest of the nation, de Gaulle fled to London. There he delivered a speech on the BBC that spread like wildfire throughout the world, sending the message that "France has lost a battle but has not lost the war." These fighting words stood in stark contrast to the swift capitulation of the French government to the Germans and propelled him to international fame. Over the next few years, he became the self-declared leader of the Free French movement, heading up the Resistance from abroad. Despite the French government's collaboration with the Germans, he brazenly demanded that France have a place at the table with the Allies. Most important, he never accepted or acknowledged France's ignominious surrender to the Nazis, upholding France's dignity during the war and afterward.

This, of course, made him a hero upon his return to France. He took full advantage of this new fame to create a prominent role for himself in postwar France. Once in the government, he became a staunchly conservative and authoritarian presence, determined to restore France's standing in the world economically and politically. He pushed to build nuclear weapons, dramatically expanded industry, turned the country's economic fortunes around, and ended the war in Algeria. His strong pro-military and anti-American stance put him at odds with much of his constituency, and he became an increasingly unpopular figure, considered by many to be intransigent and out of the step with the times.

The country erupted in rioting in 1968 that almost brought down the government. Even though the students and workers were rising up against *his* conservative, old-school policies, de Gaulle managed to quell the unrest and restore order.

De Gaulle resigned in 1969 and retired to the countryside. To many, he was a living embodiment of France, and he pursued an aggressive policy of French nationalism. This fierce pride in his country was the reason for both his rise at the outset of World War II and his decline in popularity later on, when the French were ready for more cordial relations with the world. Though he sparked no end of controversy, there's no doubt about his central role in shaping Parisians' vision of themselves and their place in the world.

M: Montparnasse-Bienvenue

Exit the metro onto the **Place du 18 Juin 1940 (1)**. The square is named in honor of the famous speech de Gaulle gave on this date via the BBC from London, in which he refused to accept the French surrender to the Nazis. He uttered what is probably the most famous line of his exceptional life: "We have lost the battle, but not the war." De Gaulle studied at the Collège Stanislaus (just northeast of the square) for a year. Head south of the Montparnasse tower into the train station and up the staircase to the left of the tracks, next to Voie 3 (Track 3). At the top, head toward the center of the rooftop, where you'll find the **Musée Jean Moulin**, which celebrates the most famous French Resistance leader of World War II, and the adjoining **Memorial Leclerc et de la Libération de Paris (2)**. These rooms are a treasure trove of information about French Resistance work during the war, with newspaper clippings, letters, photos, footage of the D-Day landings, hand-drawn sabotage plans, personal effects, and more. Retrace your steps, veer left on av. du Maine, and head west along bd. du Montparnasse, then north on bd. des Invalides. De Gaulle lived and worked in the 7th arrondissement for much of his life. As a child, he lived on av. de Breteil and on av. Duquesne and attended school off bd. Raspail, all of which are nearby. Imagine a young de Gaulle walking these streets to school—a tall, serious child, unaware that he would someday lead the country. Enter the **Hôtel des Invalides (3)** from the south. Here, you'll find three separate museums that reveal elements of de Gaulle's life. On the western edge (near the ticket lobby), the **Musée de l'Ordre de la Libération** honors Resistance fighters from the war. It contains military artifacts of all kinds (medals, maps, radio equipment, propaganda, and more). In the **Musée de l'Armée**, you'll find video footage from the war, including some of de Gaulle triumphantly marching down the Champs-Élysées after the liberation of Paris. (De Gaulle actually pressured the Allies to free Paris before they moved on to Germany.) You'll find objects belonging to de Gaulle, as well as a thorough history of the French experience during the war. Finally, in the northeast corner, the **Historial Charles de Gaulle** details not only the former president's military history, but his long and influential role as a politician shaping postwar France. Here, you'll learn about de Gaulle's role in granting Algerian independence, the inauguration of the Fifth Republic, the civil chaos of the 1968 riots, and more. Catch the metro at La Tour-Maubourg.

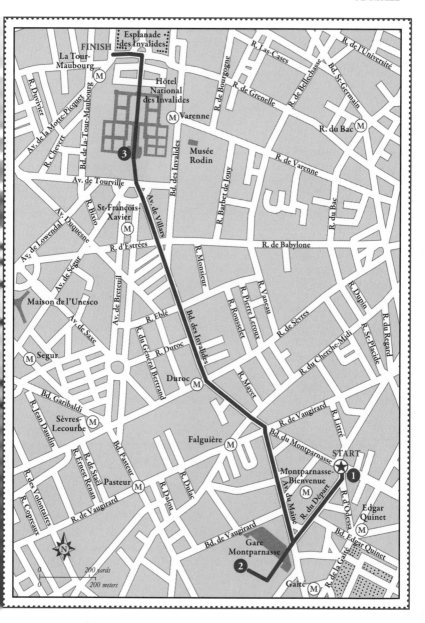

Honoré de Balzac

"I am a galley slave to pen and ink."

In the first decades of the nineteenth century, after the tumultuous French Revolution, France underwent another series of cataclysmic political changes: Napoléon rose to power, then fell from grace. The monarchy was restored, then chased out. Napoléon returned triumphant, only to crash and burn at Waterloo. The royals returned once again, and on and on. French society experienced seismic shifts as a result. Long-established social hierarchies were shaken to the core. Money became all-powerful, replacing titles as a source of status. The young and ambitious hoped to gain a foothold in the new government, but there were no longer any established procedures to follow. Society was breaking down and rebuilding itself. And Honoré de Balzac was born right into the heart of it all.

Although Balzac's early novels brought him a certain level of recognition, it was his *La Comédie Humaine*, a complex, interlinked, multivolume collection of novels, that secured his place in literary history. He studied the human animal, observing and recording its behavior and motivation much as a scientist studies animals. And what better place to observe the breadth of society than early nineteenth-century

Paris, a city surging with great wealth, grinding poverty, political turmoil, power struggles, greed, and ambition? Paris, with its staggeringly complex societal structures, provided endless fodder for *La Comédie Humaine*. A zealous—and sometimes cruel—observer of human nature, Balzac loved to bring battling social classes into play with one another: the nouveau riche vs. the old money, the young vs. the old, the aspiring vs. the established. Throughout, money—the lack of it, the desire for it, the status gained by amassing it, the subtle but prominent displays of it—was always a central theme.

Balzac's own existence was rather full of drama as well. He spent most of his life in debt, and was constantly on the move, trying to stay ahead of creditors. He lived all over Paris, rented rooms under pseudonyms, and found places with back doors so that he could flee his pursuers as they entered. Balzac's mounting debts became one of the defining elements of his intense life, and his need to make ever more money eventually drove him to the breaking point. Balzac was famous for working up to eighteen hours a day, drinking prodigious quantities of coffee to keep up his feverish pace. It's largely

believed that he died at the young age of fifty-one because he pushed himself so hard.

One of the definitive chroniclers of Paris in the first half of the nineteenth century, Balzac created an astonishingly thorough account of a time and place. But one of the reasons he is still famous today is that he went well beyond that: He brilliantly captured many of the timeless and universal aspects of human nature that we can all relate to no matter when and where we live.

M: Place Monge + metro to Passy

Head west out of place Monge on rue Ortolan and continue onto rue du Pot de Fer, then turn left to reach **30 rue Tournefort** (**1**), previously called rue Neuve-Ste-Geneviève. This building is believed to be the model for the pension in *Le Père Goriot*, the most famous novel from Balzac's *La Comédie Humaine*. To a young and aspiring Rastignac, the novel's protagonist, the street would have seemed a distant backwater at the shadowy bottom of a hill, a long way from the glamour and wealth of the Right Bank, expressing "the common sadness of a place where the houses resemble prisons and the roll of a carriage is an event." In Balzac's day, this plain building represented everything that he wanted to rise above and leave behind. The author knew this quarter well; he lived nearby on rue Cassini for several years (the building is no longer there). Head north along rue Tournefort and turn left onto rue de l'Estrapade. Head up rue Clotaire. The church where Old Goriot is taken to be buried, **St-Étienne du Mont** (**2**), is right behind the Panthéon. Head out to rue Soufflot, then turn right on rue Cousin. This is the heart of the student quarter, where ambitious youth have come for centuries to study and improve their lot in life. Cross through the student-filled plaza and turn right on rue Monsieur le Prince to reach **Polidor** (**3**; 41 rue Monsieur le Prince), a cheap and hearty student *bouillon* dating back to the 1840s, similar in ambience to Flicoteaux, the restaurant that Balzac (and several of his characters) used to frequent. Continue up to bd. St-Germain and turn left. Detour up rue de Seine and turn left to reach **17 rue Visconti** (**4**), where the author set up his own printing press in his early days. This venture landed him in serious debt, from which he never managed to free himself. Continue straight, turn left on rue Bonaparte, then right on bd. St-Germain to reach the **Musée des Lettres et Manuscrits** (**5**; 222 bd. St-Germain), where you can see one of Balzac's notebooks and various letters.

To complete this tour of Balzac's life, consider catching the metro at rue du Bac and descend at Passy in the 16th arrondissement (Balzac would have felt it important to note that this neighborhood is a bastion of "old money"). Head up rue de l'Alboni and turn left on rue Raynouard to reach the Maison de Balzac (47 rue Raynouard). Balzac lived here for eight years, toiling away feverishly on *La Comédie Humaine*. Here, you'll find his favorite coffeepot, his work area, letters, manuscripts, and personal effects. Catch the metro back at Passy.

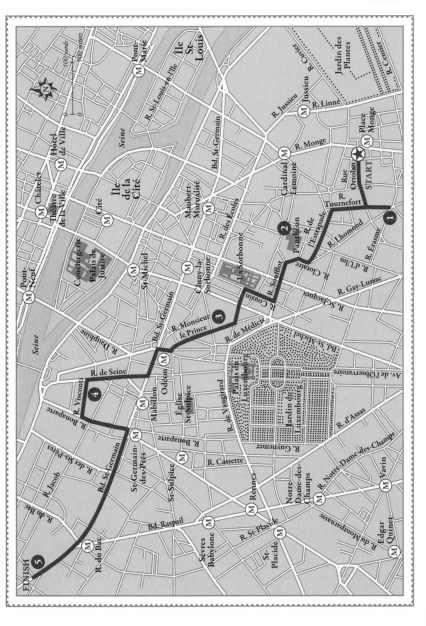

JOSEPHINE BAKER

"Paris is the dance, and I am the dancer."

The stars aligned for Josephine Baker when she first set foot in Paris in 1925. It was what the French called *le coup de foudre*—lightning love. Catapulted to instant fame with her very first performance there, she was rarely out of the limelight for the next five decades. When asked about her love of France, she was the first to admit that "France made me what I am."

Baker was born in St. Louis, Missouri, in 1906, and her childhood was nomadic, impoverished, and hard by any measure: She had her first job at the age of eight and had married twice by the age of fifteen. Despite the hard knocks, she discovered she loved performing: "Seeing everybody looking at me electrified me, as if I'd had a slug of gin." She made a name for herself based on her comic routine and captivated audiences with her charismatic, goofy energy. Meanwhile, 1920s Parisians were obsessed with everything they deemed "exotic," which included jazz, tribal art, and black performers. When an American decided to put together a black revue to perform in Paris, Baker jumped at the chance.

Baker was initially shocked when the revue's directors insisted that she appear bare breasted (which was actually fairly common in Paris at the time), but she ultimately consented. On the first night of "La Revue Nègre," she performed the finale topless, dancing to an African beat as though possessed, and the audience was mesmerized. It was a roaring success, and she became the talk of the town. She continued to reinvent herself—evolving from a comic star to a dancer to a singer—conquering the city anew time and again.

Just as Paris loved her, she fell under the spell of Paris. For the first time in her life, Baker was treated as an equal. She embraced the city's decadent nightlife scene, going out to the jazz clubs in Montmartre after her performances and staying out 'til dawn. Paris exposed her to glamour, fashion, celebrities, and artists. Once an impoverished comedic side act in a country ruled by segregation, Baker was suddenly the highest-paid entertainer in Europe. No wonder one of her most famous songs was "J'ai deux amours, mon pays et Paris"(I have two loves, my country and Paris).

World War II gave Baker the opportunity to prove her loyalty to France. Based mostly in North Africa, she became active in the French Resistance, transporting messages in invisible ink in the margins of her music. When she returned to France

in the fall of 1944, she was hailed as a heroine. She suffered many ups and downs later in her life—stomach ailments, marital difficulties, financial woes, volatile moods, eviction from her rural chateau in the Dordogne, bad press in the United States—but she always managed to rise again. Paris never tired of her, and that devotion gave her strength. She died of a stroke at the age of sixty-nine and was honored with a state funeral at la Madeleine, in the heart of the city that made her who she was.

M: Alma-Marceau

Head up av. Montaigne to the **Théâtre des Champs-Élysées** (**1;** 13 av. Montaigne). When Josephine Baker arrived in Paris for the first time in 1925, she and her group came straight to this theater. This is Paris as she first saw it—and where Paris first glimpsed her, performing her *Danse Sauvage* to such huge acclaim. Here, Baker experienced life without segregation for the first time. Turn left up rue du Boccador and right on rue de la Trémoille, where she lived with her husband, Jo Bouillon. Turn left on rue François Ier. One incarnation of her nightclub, Chez Josephine, existed along here. Veer onto av. George V, and turn right to stroll down the av. des Champs-Élysées to #77 (**2**). Baker lived here early in her career in what she called her "marble palace"—a dwelling of over-the-top splendor complete with a menagerie of wild animals, including monkeys, parrots, and her pet cheetah, Chiquita. All eyes must have been upon her as she walked the diamond-collared Chiquita down the avenue. Turn left down rue du Colisée to reach **Le Boeuf sur le Toit** (**3;** #34); it moved to this location in 1941. Le Boeuf is where Jo Bouillon worked as the club's band leader. (Inquire about their *Soirées Jazz*, evenings of live jazz that take place on Mondays.) Continue down the street and turn right down rue du Faubourg St-Honoré, then left on rue Royale to reach **la Madeleine** (**4**), where Baker received a state burial thanks to her service in the French Resistance during World War II. Veer right up bd. des Capucines and settle in at the timelessly elegant **Café de la Paix** (**5;** 12 bd. des Capucines), another of Baker's favorite spots. Catch the metro at Opéra.

Bonus: For a glamorous evening in true Josephine Baker style, pay tribute to the star with dinner at La Coupole (102 bd. du Montparnasse), one of her very favorite places: She used to dance the night away in the basement here. (A square a few blocks from here was named in her honor in 2001.) Alternatively, enjoy an evening of jazz (Duc des Lombards, 42 rue des Lombards, 1st arr., is considered one of the best spots in town to hear it), or splash out on a night of glitz and dancing at the Folies Bergère (32 rue Richer), another place where Baker performed on and off for many years. Alternatively, head north to the Montmartre area. Baker used to frequent the Art Deco shrine Aromatik (7 rue Jean Baptiste, 9th arrondissement); it's just steps from where her nightclub, Chez Josephine, was located (40 rue Fontaine) and is still a cabaret to this day.

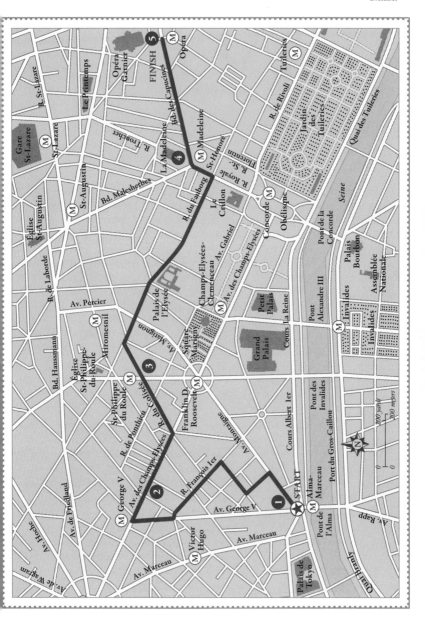

SIMONE DE BEAUVOIR & JEAN-PAUL SARTRE

"Everything has been figured out, except how to live."
— JEAN-PAUL SARTRE

"Change your life today. Don't gamble on the future, act now, without delay."
— SIMONE DE BEAUVOIR

Simone de Beauvoir and Jean-Paul Sartre, the darlings of the intellectual movement and luminaries of Saint Germain, first met in 1929. Both were studying for the philosophy exam that would enable them to become professors. Sartre won first prize, and de Beauvoir came in second; at age twenty-one, she was the youngest person ever to pass. Thus began a lifelong connection that shaped not only contemporary philosophy, but also the neighborhood of Saint Germain, which the two staked out as their spiritual home.

They became lovers, but never married. After passing their exams, they took teaching positions in other parts of France, but they soon returned to Paris, where Sartre continued teaching. They lived modestly in small hotels and studios in the neighborhood and feverishly pursued their shared, true professional goal—writing.

Sartre's first novel, *La Nausée*, was published in 1938 to great acclaim. In this and his other early books, he delivered crushing opinions on bourgeois life and promoted his philosophy of individual freedom. His writing career was temporarily put on hold by World War II, during which he was drafted and was held as a prisoner of war in Germany. When he was released in 1941, he returned to Paris and gave up teaching altogether to devote himself to writing full-time. De Beauvoir's work wasn't published until 1943, and she finally received the recognition she deserved with the publication of *Les Mandarins* in 1954, which won the prestigious Prix Goncourt.

By the end of the war, Sartre and de Beauvoir were the royalty of Saint Germain, and they remained very much in the public eye for years afterward. They could usually be found working away at their favorite cafés, debating with other writers and philosophers, attending communist rallies, and generally changing people's thinking on marriage, life, love, war, feminism, the rights of individuals, and more. Though Sartre continued to embrace individual freedom,

he became increasingly left-leaning, embracing social responsibility and favoring communism. (At one point, he was on the verge of being arrested for civil disobedience, when President de Gaulle stepped in and said, "You don't arrest Voltaire.") Meanwhile, de Beauvoir's *The Second Sex* was published in 1949, which propelled her to the forefront of the feminist movement.

Their philosophy gave Parisian youth a sense of hope and freedom after the horrors of the war. The younger generation wanted to put the past firmly behind them and embraced the new thinking espoused by de Beauvoir and Sartre. Emulating their leaders became their ideal, and being an intellectual became *de rigueur*—as did looking the part.

Young Parisians donned black, sat in smoky cafés, and rebelled against the strictures of the past. What began as a starkly intellectual philosophy morphed into a full-blown bohemian lifestyle. Saint Germain was *the* place to be, and would never be the same again.

Both de Beauvoir and Sartre moved on to Montparnasse, where they lived in apartments at opposite ends of the cemetery. Though they had ended their romantic relationship long before, their intellectual bond and friendship remained strong until the end. They wrote, worked, and spent time together up until Sartre died in 1980. De Beauvoir followed in 1986. They are buried side by side at Montparnasse Cemetery.

M: St-Michel

Head west out of the Place St-Michel on rue St-André des Arts, which turns into rue de Buci. At rue de Seine, turn left. The **Hôtel Louisiane** (**1**; 56 rue de Seine) was home to Sartre and de Beauvoir for three years starting in 1943. De Beauvoir later said, "I'd never lodged anywhere that fulfilled my dreams as that place did; I would have happily stayed there for the rest of my life." Backtrack, and continue on rue de Buci, then turn right on bd. St-Germain to reach the famed **Deux Magots** (**2**; 6 pl. St-Germain-des-Prés), which became ground zero for the Existentialist movement once Sartre and de Beauvoir started working there. Hemingway, Joyce, Camus, Picasso, and countless other luminaries have spent time here. At the north end of the square is **42 rue Bonaparte** (**3**), where Sartre lived cozily with his mother for many years. The apartment was actually bombed twice by those who wanted to silence Sartre's vocal political opinions. Alternatively, head down to **Café de Flore** (**4**; 172 bd. St-Germain), which served as something of a spiritual home to both writers. Here they wrote, debated, drank, and socialized, transforming it into the bohemian and intellectual magnet that it still is today. Glamorous as it is now, the draw to de Beauvoir and Sartre in the 1940s was more utilitarian: The café was always well heated (which couldn't be said for the drafty little rooms they occupied nearby). De Beauvoir preferred working upstairs, especially during World War II, when the Germans took over the terrace below.

Head south on rue de Rennes. Veer left on bd. Raspail. At bd. du Montparnasse, turn right to view **#103** (**5**), where de Beauvoir was born and grew up in great comfort. Continue down bd. Raspail, veering right onto rue Schoelcher. With the successful publication of *Les Mandarins*, de Beauvoir was finally able to buy her own apartment at **#11bis** (**6**), and this is where she spent the last thirty-three years of her life. Continue south and turn right on rue Froidevaux. Enter the Cimetière du Montparnasse at the end of the street and head north, then right to reach their **gravesite** (**7**). Exit onto bd. Edgar Quinet; Sartre spent his final years at #29. He regularly walked along here on his way to and from de Beauvoir's apartment, stopping at the Café Liberté (1 rue de la Gaîté) on his way home from her place in the morning. Cross onto sq. Delambre, and turn right on rue Delambre. Stop for a *café* at **Le Dôme** (**8**; 108 bd. du Montparnasse), their daily headquarters in their early years. Catch the metro at Vavin.

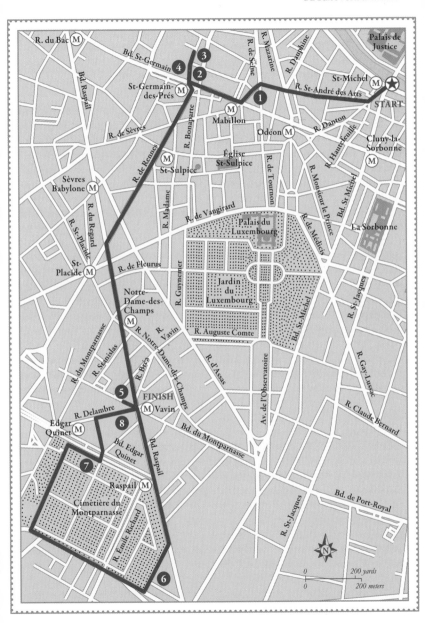

Henri de Toulouse-Lautrec

"I have tried to depict the true and not the ideal."

Henri de Toulouse-Lautrec was born in 1864 into an aristocratic family in the south of France. He loved drawing from an early age and was fortunate to have parents who actually encouraged his sketching. Probably the most defining aspect of Toulouse-Lautrec's childhood was a genetic disorder that left him with child-length legs and a man-size torso as an adult. Because of this, he steered clear of most typical childhood activities and retreated increasingly into his art. At the age of eighteen, he escaped the confines of the countryside and moved up to Paris, where he settled in the heart of bohemian Montmartre and studied painting formally at the prestigious École des Beaux Arts.

Montmartre teemed with all kinds of life in the late nineteenth century. Artists and writers squatted in the tiny studios and garrets perched on the steep, labyrinthine slopes of this village-within-a-city. Brothels, cabarets, dancing halls, bars, cafés, and other gathering places sprang up to cater to the many young, single men who colonized the area. Toulouse-Lautrec wasted no time becoming a regular at many of these establishments. With his dry wit, he was often the life of the party. Living in Montmartre, he also befriended other influential artists, among them Degas, who lived next door to him for a while, and Van Gogh.

Ultimately, Paris gave Toulouse-Lautrec the key to his art: material. Despite (or perhaps because of) his aristocratic roots, he developed an affinity for the squalid and degenerate underbelly of urban life. Depicting the city's hidden side became his life's work. Inspired by urban nightlife and fascinated by the people working within it, he never shied away from the tawdriness, exhaustion, or sheer banality lurking behind the superficial glamour. He frequented brothels, often residing with the prostitutes for long periods, and some of his most famous works are his intimate portraits of them in casually reclining poses.

His lasting legacy is, of course, his poster work for the cabarets in Montmartre. With his first exuberant poster of La Goulue kicking up her skirt at the Moulin Rouge, he revolutionized publicity. Although other artists diminished his artistic achievements in that arena, claiming they weren't true art, Toulouse-Lautrec didn't care. He was painting the life he knew so well—and in the process he created some of the most

lasting and well-known images of Parisian life ever made.

His mantra, "one should not drink much, but often," caught up with him at an early age. Unfortunately, he indulged with incre asing frequency in the decadent nightlife he loved so well. He was unable to tame his rampant alcoholism, his artwork suffered, and he was forced to leave Paris. He spent time in a sanatorium, suffering delusions of persecution, and eventually died of syphilis and alcoholism at the age of thirty-six on his family estate. Although he didn't live long enough to know it, he is now considered one of the masters of Post-Impressionism, and he captured the spirit of the city during its heyday.

M: Pigalle

Head south down rue Jean-Baptiste Pigalle, and turn right up rue Pierre Fontaine. The artist lived in **four different apartments** (1) on this street. You'll find a plaque at #19, but he also lived at #19bis, #21, and #30; Degas lived here, too, and became an artistically influential friend. (Pop into sweets shop L'Étoile d'Or on the ground floor of #30—their Bernachon chocolate is considered some of the finest in the world.) Continue up the street to bd. de Clichy, cross the street, and turn left to pay homage at the hard-to-miss **Moulin Rouge** (2), one of the artist's favorite haunts and the inspiration for his legendary poster featuring the dancer La Goulue. Now something of a tourist trap, it was once a symbol of Paris's louche glamour. It still puts on dinner-and-dance shows, and within, you'll find the artist's original posters adorning the red walls. Backtrack and turn left on rue Lepic, which turns left. Veer right up the hill. Turn left on rue Tourlaque. Look up to view the artist's fifth-floor studio on the corner on the far side of rue Caulaincourt, at #7 (3), which he kept for twelve years. Here, Suzanne Valadon modeled for him (and later became his mistress), and he created his legendary posters. Backtrack and continue up rue Lepic to the **Moulin de la Galette** (4; 83 rue Lepic), another of his favorite dance halls. Imagine Toulouse-Lautrec making this trek up the hill each evening, drunkenly stumbling back down in the wee hours. The cabaret and nightlife here served as an inspiration to several artists: Van Gogh and Renoir were also frequent patrons. (It's still open daily for lunch and dinner.) Continue uphill and veer left. Turn right on rue Norvins, then left on rue des Saules and right up pretty rue Cortot to reach the **Musée de Montmartre** (5; 12 rue Cortot). The photos, maps, paintings, and posters here reveal the history of the neighborhood that was central to Toulouse-Lautrec's life and work. Continue up the street and turn right on rue du Mont-Cenis to reach the restaurant-lined place du Tertre, where today's local artists ply their trade. **La Maison Catherine** (6; 6 pl. du Tertre), on site since 1793, has fed many of the starving artists who once lived in the area. Head east toward Sacré-Coeur. Take the funicular down or walk down the much-photographed staircase to the right of it. Continue straight to reach bd. de Rochechouart, passing the **Élysée Montmartre** (7; 72 bd. de Rochechouart), another favorite cabaret of the artist. Catch the metro at Anvers.

Bonus: To complete your tour, pay a visit to the Musée d'Orsay.

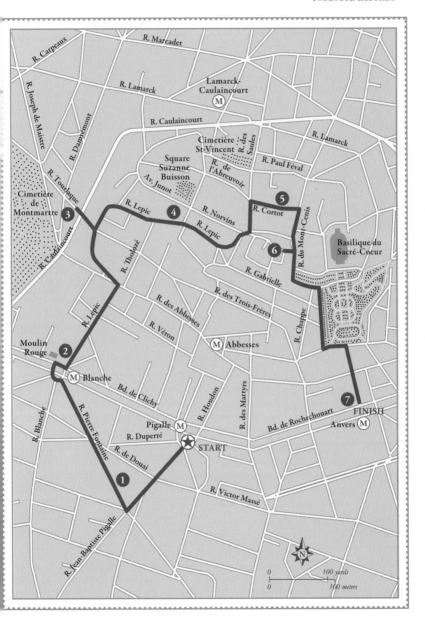

Julia Child

"I am half-French and that is all there is to it."

"Gee whizz, what a city," Julia Child wrote to her friend Avis DeVoto in 1955. "Why live anywhere else is the eternal question." For Child, Paris was the city that changed everything. She didn't pursue the culinary arts until she lived there in her thirties, but once she discovered her calling, she embraced it with passion, determination, and formidable energy.

Julia Child arrived in France for the first time in 1948 at the age of thirty-six. Her husband, Paul—part of the American diplomatic corps—was assigned to Paris. She and Paul drove off from the port at Le Havre in their large, sky-blue station wagon and stopped for lunch in Rouen. This first meal—a simple but expertly prepared sole meunière—was a revelation for Child. French food was like nothing she'd ever tasted. In their first apartment in Paris, she started cooking on her own, initially as a cost-saving measure. But she found she enjoyed it. She befriended the merchants on her street, watched how her neighbors shopped, and learned to speak French along the way. Her favorite vegetable merchant on the rue de Bourgogne taught her "all about shallots, and how to tell a good potato from a bad one. She took great pleasure in instructing me about which vegetables were best

to eat, and when; and how to prepare them correctly." At her *crémerie*, she marveled at the owner's "ability to calibrate a cheese's readiness down to the hour." She explained, "The Parisian grocers insisted that I interact with them personally. . . . They certainly made me work for my supper, but, oh, what suppers!"

When she decided the time had come to get some serious training, Child signed up for courses at Le Cordon Bleu. Upon graduating, she banded together with two French friends to open a small cooking school for Americans. Fortuitously, these friends eventually asked for her help with a French cookbook intended for American audiences. She threw herself headlong into the project. And that was it. She had found her calling.

Over the next few years, Child would spend countless hours developing the book's recipes. No detail was too small. She worked on mayonnaise until she got the perfect foolproof recipe; she tasted every bouillabaisse in Marseille to understand all the possible variations on the dish; she studied the difference between French and American flour; she simply would not give up until she got it all right.

It took nearly a decade for *Mastering the Art of French Cooking* to be

published, but once it was, in 1961, Child's life changed forever. She became a huge celebrity, hosting a television series that brought her ever-lasting fame. Before Julia Child, the culinary landscape of the United States had been utterly barren. In an era when Americans were consumed by speed and convenience, Child was absorbing the classic principles of French cuisine:

"If one doesn't use the freshest ingredients, or read the whole recipe before starting, and if one rushes through the cooking, the result will be an inferior taste and texture." Child bravely and brazenly flew in the face of the trend of the times, insisting that cooking was an art that deserved to be celebrated. In doing so, she forever changed the way Americans cooked.

M: École Militaire

Head up av. La Motte Piquet and veer left onto rue Cler. This was Julia Child's shopping street, and it's still lined with old-school butchers, bakers, and the like. The shops here were Child's first culinary training ground. It was here that she first grasped the idea that excellent ingredients are an essential prerequisite to serious cooking. She also learned that the trick to successful shopping was "not to rush, push too hard, or take people's goodwill for granted." Stop for lunch at well-loved **Café du Marché** (**1**; 38 rue Cler). Turn right on rue St-Dominique. Turn left on rue Jean Nicot to visit **Bellota Bellota** (**2**; 18 rue Jean Nicot), which specializes in Spanish hams and cheese. Backtrack and continue along rue St-Dominique. Turn left on rue de Bourgogne (where Child shopped daily). Turn right on rue de l'Université. Child lived with her husband Paul at #81 (**3**). Despite the traditional exterior, the interior was quite eccentrically decorated and furnished. It was in this kitchen that she first started experimenting— and soon became obsessed. She described the space as "light and airy," with an immense stove, a minuscule oven, and only cold running water. Continue north on rue de Bourgogne and turn right on quai Anatole France; Child herself loved to stroll along here, "poking my nose into shops and asking the merchants about everything." Continue straight, then cross the Seine at the Pont des Arts. Cross through the Cour Carrée du Louvre, turn right on rue de Rivoli, then left on rue du Louvre, and right on rue Coquillière to reach **E. Dehillerin** (**4**; 18 rue Coquillière), Child's favorite shop. She described it as "*the* kitchen store of all time . . . stuffed with an infinite number of wondrous gadgets, tools, implements, and geegaws." It is still a warren of narrow aisles brimming with cooking gadgets of every kind—whisks in a dozen sizes, baking molds, copper pots, knives, and more. Once you've reached saturation point, step over to **Au Pied de Cochon** (**5**; 6 rue Coquillière) where, Child says, "As dawn lightened the edges of the sky, we found ourselves . . . for a traditional bowl of onion soup, glasses of red wine, and cups of coffee. At five-fifteen, we straggled home." Why not do the same? Catch the metro at Les Halles.

Bonus: To further experience Child's Paris, book a table at Brasserie Lapp, Laperouse (where she celebrated her fortieth birthday) or le Grand Vefour (where she regularly had lunch). Two of the best open-air markets are the Marché du Président Wilson (Wednesday, Saturday) and Marché Raspail (Sunday for organic-only). The Cordon Bleu offers classes to visitors as well.

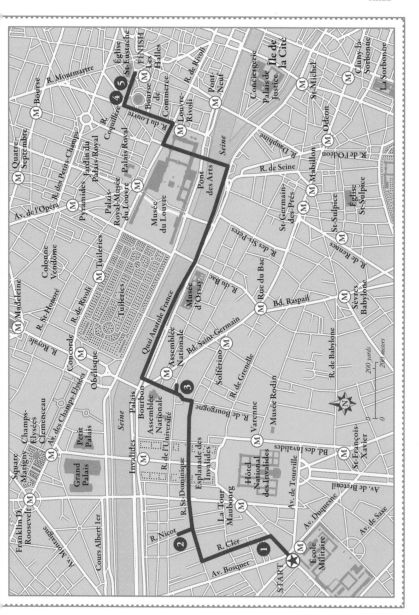

ÉMILE ZOLA

*"I am little concerned with beauty or perfection. . . .
All I care about is life, struggle, intensity."*

Émile Zola came of age during a time of dizzying change in Paris. Baron Haussmann had just swept through with his renovation of Paris, converting intimate lanes into gleaming grand boulevards; the first department stores were changing the commercial landscape; the food market at Les Halles sparkled with new iron-and-glass arcades. Though thrilling in many respects, this new era disrupted long-established social norms and upended traditional ways. A perceptive and ruthlessly honest Zola witnessed it all and recorded it for posterity.

Zola was born in Paris, spent his childhood outside the city, and then returned to Paris at the age of eighteen, where he lived in poverty in various drafty garrets around the Latin Quarter. Having failed his French baccalaureate exams (surprisingly, more than once), he worked at a bookstore and began writing. Although he initially wrote in the style of the Romantics, he abandoned its trademark sentiment in favor of what came to be called the Naturalist style. Contrary to the outdoorsy connotation of the word, the hallmark of the movement was a focus on controversial social issues, featuring squalid, industrial, distinctly urban settings

as backdrops. Zola described his approach as scientific rather than romantic. His descriptions were cruelly realistic and brutally unsympathetic. Zola wanted to capture the gritty reality of urban life and to expose the effects of the Industrial Age on the social hierarchy. And given the all-day (and all-night) activity in the city all around him, he certainly had plenty of material to work with.

Zola came to fame with the publication of *L'Assommoir*, which scandalized Paris with its exposé of an impoverished and alcoholic Parisian washerwoman. He followed with *Nana* (daughter of the washerwoman), which depicts in provocative detail the rise and fall of a Parisian courtesan. He tackled the plight of the working classes in his epic *Germinal*, a harrowing account of life in the French coal mines. Another classic, *The Belly of Paris*, covers the inner machinations of the wholesale food market formerly located at Les Halles. He exposed the Parisian arts scene in *The Masterpiece* (losing his good friend Paul Cezanne in the process).

Up until 1898, Zola was merely one of France's greatest writers. All that changed when he published a letter

titled "J'Accuse!" in a city paper. In it he took a stand in the controversial Dreyfus Affair. (In 1894, the French government had unjustly convicted Jewish officer Alfred Dreyfus of treason. When new evidence came to light that would have exonerated him, the government covered it up.) Zola's letter, in which he accused the government of anti-semitism and helped spread the news of the cover-up, opened up the scandal anew. As a result, the case was reopened, and Dreyfus was released. For his efforts, Zola was charged with libel, and he fled the country to avoid prosecution until the charges were dropped.

Zola died a few years later from carbon monoxide poisoning. Whether this was the result of an accident or malicious intent has never been resolved. He is buried in the Panthéon.

M: Blanche

Zola lived in different parts of Paris over the course of his life, but spent most of his time in some half dozen apartments in this northern part of the city. Head north up rue Lepic and turn right onto **rue Véron (1)** to view the street where Zola's character Nana resided. It was once the city's Red Light District, and Zola relished describing it in all its tawdriness. Retrace your steps and head southwest on rue de Bruxelles to **#21bis (2)**, one of Zola's many residences. This is where he wrote the famous letter "J'accuse!" condemning the French government's handling of the Dreyfus Affair. It is also where he died of carbon monoxide poisoning. Turn left at the end on place Adolphe Max and left again on rue Ballu, where Zola lived briefly in a handsome building at **#23 (3)**. Continue straight, jog right at rue Blanche onto rue Chaptal. Jog up rue Pigalle, then turn right on rue Victor Massé and right on rue des Martyrs. Today, this shopping street teems with baby strollers and young families; back in Zola's day, however, it was home to several lesbian bars and frequented by those "down on their luck." Turn left on rue de Châteaudun and right on rue Le Peletier. Imagine it as Nana saw it: "the last open market for the contracts of a night." Turn right on bd. Haussmann. These imposing boulevards were the embodiment of the new Paris and its leap into the modern world. Turn left on rue Scribe, passing near the **Grands Magasins (4),** Paris's two main department stores. Zola made them a centerpiece in his novel *Au Bonheur des Dames*. By revealing the new department stores' inner workings, he touched on many social issues of the time: the rise of a consumer culture and the changing role of women, among others. Veer left on rue Auber and stop for a drink at **Café de la Paix (5**; 12 bd. des Capucines), one of the author's frequent watering holes. Head east on rue du 4 Septembre. You'll pass **rue de Choiseul (6)**, the setting for the *Pot-Bouille (Stew Pot)*, another story of class that examines the social dynamics of several families who have moved into a new apartment building (a relatively new concept at the time) on this street. Turn right on rue Montorgueil, the setting of *The Belly of Paris*. To picture what it looked like back then, loop around to **Cochon à l'Oreille (7**; 15 rue Montmartre), a historic bistro that dates back to the area's heyday as a market center. You'll find ceramic tiles depicting old market scenes along the walls, an apt place to sit down and celebrate Zola's work. Catch the metro at Les Halles.

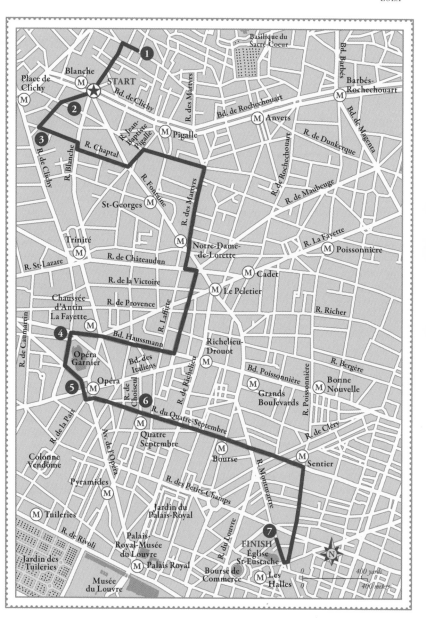

⨍UGUSTE ⨍RODIN

*"What is commonly called ugliness in nature
can in art become full of great beauty."*

When Rodin debuted his sculpture of a life-sized male nude titled *The Age of Bronze* in Brussels in 1877, it was so realistic that critics speculated that he must have cast it from a live model; they simply didn't believe that he could possibly have sculpted it himself.

In fact, given Rodin's enduring fame, it's perhaps surprising that his career got off to such a slow and rocky start. He was rejected *three* times by the École des Beaux Arts (the entrance committee thought his sculpting style strayed too far from the classical idealism that was the norm at the time). To make a living, he worked as a hired mason by day, with only the early mornings and late evenings to devote to his art. Throughout his early life, Rodin often had only a few *sous* to his name, and endured long bouts of hunger and cold in drafty, unheated studios. Still, Rodin felt compelled to persevere, driven by an almost compulsive need to fulfill his artistic vision.

Intense and singularly driven, Rodin pursued sculpting despite the many hardships this career path entailed. He began drawing as a child and showed an early aptitude for sculpting at the Petite École in the Latin Quarter. As soon as he tried it, he knew he'd found his life's calling. He studied the volume, shape, and depth of everything around him. He tracked down books on Michelangelo at the Bibliothèque Nationale, attended anatomy lectures, visited galleries, and took classes wherever he could. Meanwhile, he toiled away in his little spare time, imbuing his pieces with such breathtaking realism that critics were affronted. One of his first pieces, *Mask of the Man with the Broken Nose*, was poorly received because the damaged form it depicted did not conform to traditional ideals of beauty.

Eventually, Rodin's fortunes turned around. With the support of testimonials from other renowned sculptors and friends who'd witnessed him working on *The Age of Bronze*, he managed to clear his name, and the sculpture was displayed at the Paris Salon in 1880. It won a gold medal. From that point forward, Rodin had plenty of work. The state commissioned him to start work on a set of doors for a future decorative arts museum (which never opened), and the result was *The Gates of Hell*. Parts of that monumental work (namely, *The Thinker* and *The Kiss*) were to become independent sculptures in

their own right and some of his best-known works. Soon he was accepting important commissions for sculptures of France's greatest celebrities.

His realistic approach continued to shock some. He originally wanted to depict Victor Hugo, France's greatest writer, in the nude (this version was turned down), and his unconventional portrait of Balzac (depicting an impassioned, haunted genius clothed in his trademark dressing gown) caused a scandal and was also rejected by the state (though today it stands prominently at the corner of bd. Montparnasse and rue Vavin).

Ultimately, despite it all, Rodin triumphed, ushering in a new era of realism and definitively altering the world's view of sculpture.

M: PLACE D'ITALIE

Head north on av. des Gobelins to reach the **Théâtre des Gobelins** (1; #73). The façade was sculpted by a young Rodin when he worked for hire as a decorative arts sculptor. (Haussmann, with his grand urban plans, created plenty of work in this department.) Continue straight onto rue Mouffetard. Rodin lived at **7 rue de l'Arbalète** (2) as a child. Back in the 1840s, this was a poor and overcrowded neighborhood. Imagine a young Rodin attending the St-Médard church at the foot of rue Mouffetard with his mother and older sister, going to school in the shadow of the nearby Val de Grace, and attending classes at the Manufacture des Gobelins. In fact, he lived all over this part of the Latin Quarter, inhabiting apartments on rue de la Tombe d'Issoire and rue des Fossés St-Jacques just southwest of here, among others. His first small studio was located just a few blocks south. Backtrack and head up rue Lhomond, veer left, turn right on rue St-Jacques (Rodin also lived on this street), and left on rue des Écoles. Continue straight onto rue de l'École de Médecine, where the **École Impériale de Dessin** (3), dubbed the Petite École, was located. Rodin began studying here at the age of fourteen and stayed for three years. This was where he first discovered sculpting. Continue up the street to Odéon, then loop around and head south down rue de l'Odéon. Veer right onto rue St-Sulpice and continue west along rue du Vieux Colombier, then rue de Sèvres. Turn right on bd. Raspail, then left on rue de Varenne to reach the **Musée Rodin** (4; 77 rue de Varenne). This is, of course, the best place to experience the sculptor's genius. You'll find his works both inside the building and in the lovely gardens. Even if you are already familiar with his pieces, their emotional impact in person is surprisingly powerful. The building was Rodin's home and studio for the last ten years of his life. He shared the space with other artists, including Matisse. When the building—a former hotel—was going to be torn down, Rodin negotiated a deal, agreeing to bequeath his works to the state if he could be allowed to remain there for the rest of his life. The deal was done, and the building, a work of art in itself, was turned into the museum it is today. Catch the metro at Varenne.

Bonus: Those interested in seeing where Rodin's other studio was should head north on rue de Bourgogne (where he lived for five years at #71), then turn left on rue de l'Université. The French state provided him with a studio at the Dépôt des Marbres at #182.

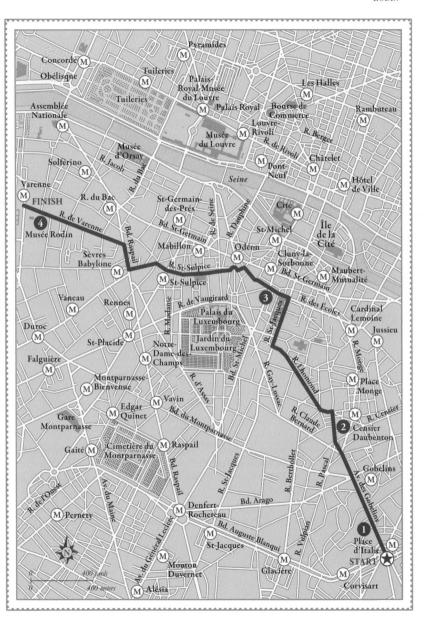

MOLIÈRE

"The duty of comedy is to correct men by amusing them."

"Writing is like prostitution.
First you do it for love, and then for a few close friends,
and then for money."

"I assure you that a learned fool is more foolish than an ignorant fool."

Known for his prodigious wit, Molière is equally famous for his shameless skewering of the upper classes. Though devilishly skilled at pointing out the buffoonery of the rich, he was also an astute observer of human nature. Buried amid all the jokes were kernels of truth about the cynical motivations of human beings and the follies of Parisian society.

Becoming France's most celebrated playwright was hardly a natural trajectory for young Molière. For one thing, he was born into a family of upholsterers in Paris, and it was assumed that he would simply carry on the business. Second, there was only one permanent theater in Paris when Molière was growing up in the first half of the seventeenth century, so few Parisians were ever exposed to any acting at all. He was fortunate to have a grandfather who loved the theater and who brought him regularly to performances. He was instantly hooked and sought out theater in any form in the city—watching, for example, the street performers who plied their trade on the Pont Neuf near his house.

Despite a dearth of theaters in his early life, Molière was fortunate to come of age during a Golden Age in France. Louis XIV actively supported the arts, Cardinal Richelieu was busy building royal theaters and gallery spaces, and theater blossomed thanks to their influence. All the same, Molière's career got off to a rocky start—the first theater troupe he led dissolved when Molière went to prison (briefly) for amassing debts. He left for the countryside, where he toured as part of an itinerant troupe for the following twelve years. But he knew he would never make a name for himself in the provinces, so he returned to Paris, the influential center of the artistic world. There, he eventually managed to perform one of his comedies before the king himself.

Although he still attracted no end of controversy (riling up the upper classes that he mocked so adeptly, as well as the Catholic Church, which spent a great deal of time trying to get his plays banned), he succeeded in securing the lifelong protection of

Louis XIV, even being granted permanent use of one of the royal theaters. Although Molière was brazen about his attacks on a wide array of social mores, he quite strategically never criticized the monarchy itself. With the king's support, his success as a playwright was guaranteed. He wrote, acted, directed, and devoted his life to the theater until his death, which occurred only hours after an evening of acting in *Le Malade Imaginaire*, in 1673. As he said himself, "We die only once, and for such a long time."

M: Palais Royal–Musée du Louvre

As you emerge from the metro, you'll come upon the imposing **Théâtre de la Comédie Française** (1), which will forever be associated with Molière. Molière's troupe became part of the Comédie Française when Louis XIV established it as the national theater in 1680. His final performance was at the Palais Royal. During a performance of *Le Malade Imaginaire* (Molière played the lead) the exhausted playwright and performer suddenly fell ill. He made it through the performance, but died later that night, likely of a pulmonary infection, at his home nearby on rue de Richelieu. On the west side of the Comédie Française, you'll find a small gift shop that carries copies of Molière's plays and theatrical memorabilia. Head north up to **40 rue de Richelieu** (2) to view the location of the building where he died (this is a more recent construction). At the head of the street named in his honor is a rather imposing **statue of the playwright** (3). Backtrack and head east along rue St-Honoré. Molière was born at the location at **#96** (4), where you'll find a plaque. Turn up rue Sauval and cut across Les Halles. Ahead is **Église St-Eustache** (5), where Molière was baptized and buried in the dark of night amidst much controversy. As an actor, he had been automatically excommunicated from the church, but he was too famous not to be given some kind of burial; his remains were later transferred to the Cimetière du Père Lachaise. Just beyond the church, turn up rue Montorgueil, then turn right on rue Mauconseil to reach the street where the **Hôtel de Bourgogne** (6), the first permanent theater in Paris, was once located. A young Molière often made this same trek with his grandfather. Backtrack to rue Montorgueil and head straight south, across Les Halles, down rue du Pont Neuf, then cross the **Pont Neuf** (7). Molière used to come here to watch street performers as a child—another defining experience that shaped his future. Cross straight onto rue Dauphine, which will lead you to the aptly named rue de l'Ancienne Comédie (the Comédie Française used to be located here). Stop at **Le Procope** (8; 13 rue de l'Ancienne Comédie), once a frequent haunt of the playwright; it was the city's first literary café and has fastidiously maintained its historic ambience. Although Molière grew up on the Right Bank, he spent a good deal of time on this side of the river. He went to school at what is now the Lycée Louis-le-Grand near the Panthéon and later embarked on his theatrical career with a troupe that practiced on the nearby rue de Seine. Catch the metro at Odéon.

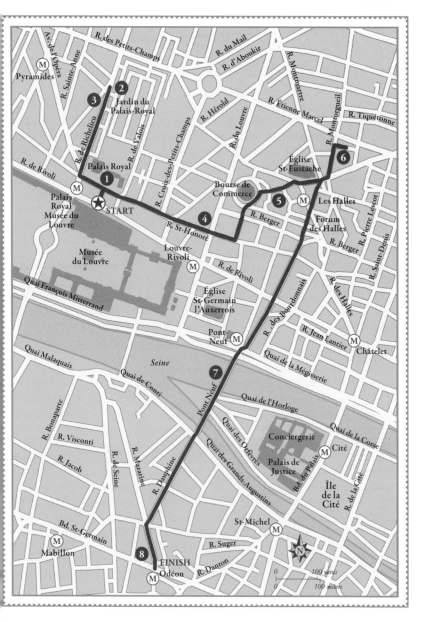

Henri Cartier-Bresson

"Photography is not documentary, but intuition, a poetic experience."

One of the world's first photojournalists, Henri Cartier-Bresson is also the undisputed master of the form. Although many of his most famous shots were taken far from Paris—in India, China, and beyond—Cartier-Bresson was heavily influenced by the city where he was raised.

Born in 1908, Cartier-Bresson grew up in the comfortable 8th arrondissement. He developed an early interest in art and spent many hours of his childhood at the Louvre. During his adolescence, he began to study art formally in Montparnasse. There, at the Académie Lhote, he studied the masters and gained an appreciation for composition, which would have a tremendous influence on his photography later on. (In fact, he was so adept at photographic composition that he hardly cropped a single photo during his entire career.)

Around this time, he ventured out into the city's cafés and took up with the Surrealists, among them André Breton and Louis Aragon. Hanging out with these avant-garde thinkers liberated him from his traditional and conservative upbringing. As he explains, "I was marked, not by Surrealist painting, but by the conceptions of Breton . . . the role of spontaneous expression and of intuition and, above all, the attitude of revolt." He began to read extensively, delving into the works of Dostoevsky, Proust, and Joyce. Having spent his entire childhood bound by the rigid confines of tradition, he was at last emboldened to embrace the unconventional. Ultimately, this mix of influences helped shape his photographic style: Through his traditional artistic training, he developed an eye for composition, while the Surrealists encouraged him to look at the world in new ways, to capture the unexpected in daily life. A photographer was born.

In his twenties, Cartier-Bresson started taking pictures casually. He moved to Africa for a while, and worked briefly in documentary film. Upon his return, he saw a photo taken by Martin Munkácsi called *Three Boys at Lake Tanganyika*. Through this image, he grasped the power of photography, and he felt compelled to pick up his camera professionally. With the advent of World War II, his newfound career shuddered to a temporary halt: He was captured and held as a POW for three years. He escaped on his third attempt. After the war, he joined forces with the legendary Robert Capa, with whom he founded Magnum Photos. He traveled the world extensively for the next twenty-five years, and became famous for capturing "the decisive moment."

His photos of world events—Gandhi hours before he died, the victory of the Communists in China, the 1968 riots in Paris—and his portraits often became the definitive visual record of those events.

Cartier-Bresson retired from photography in 1973. He settled permanently back in Paris, in a top-floor apartment on the rue de Rivoli. There, he put his camera down once and for all and returned to what he claimed was his first and only true love: painting. For the next thirty years, he hardly snapped a photo, instead spending his days at the Louvre or on his terrace, sketching. He died in 2004, having practically single-handedly transformed photojournalism during his lifetime.

M: Gaîté + metro from Montparnasse to St-Germain-des-Prés

Head south on av. du Maine, turn right on rue de l'Ouest, left on rue Lebouis, and left on impasse Lebouis to reach the diminutive but luminous **Fondation Henri Cartier-Bresson (1)**. The foundation hosts three rotating exhibits of various photographers' work each year, but one floor is devoted to the work of Cartier-Bresson himself. There you'll find a dozen of his photographs, including the iconic *Behind the Gare St-Lazare*. You'll also see his famous Leica and its case (a remarkably small and simple-looking apparatus) as well as a collection of his books. It's an excellent, quiet space in which to learn more about the jaw-droppingly wide range of his work. Backtrack to av. du Maine and head north to the metro. Although Montparnasse is not especially scenic, Cartier-Bresson spent several years in this part of town taking art classes and gathering with the Surrealists, who had staked out their turf nearby. (The Café du Dôme on bd. Montparnasse was a regular haunt during those early days.) Take the metro directly from Montparnasse to St-Germain-des-Prés. (You will pass the Gaîté metro station on your way, but continue on to Montparnasse to avoid having to transfer.) Stop in for coffee at the **Café de Flore (2;** 172 bd. St-Germain), where Cartier-Bresson once met up with his fellow POWs after World War II. Head up rue Bonaparte and cross the **Pont des Arts (3)**; it was here that he took what would become the definitive portrait of Jean-Paul Sartre. Cross over to the **Louvre (4)**, where Cartier-Bresson spent much of his time drawing after he'd retired from photography. Turn left down rue de Rivoli to pass the building he lived in for many years at **#198 (5)**. His apartment overlooked the Tuileries, and he used to sketch the gardens from his terrace. Although Cartier-Bresson traveled extensively during his career, he always returned here. If any place was ever truly home to the peripatetic photographer, this was it. Turn right on rue de Castiglione, head through the Place Vendôme, continue up rue de la Paix, and turn left on rue Daunou. Enjoy a drink at the **Hôtel Scribe (6;** 1 rue Scribe), where Cartier-Bresson feted the liberation of Paris with his longtime friend and colleague Robert Capa (and the rest of the press corps), who declared that he was all too happy to be an out-of-work war photographer. Cartier-Bresson spent his childhood years just northwest of here, in a comfortable bourgeois apartment at 31 rue de Lisbonne, and attended several schools just down the street (Lycée Condorcet and École Fenelon) as a child. Catch the metro at Opéra.

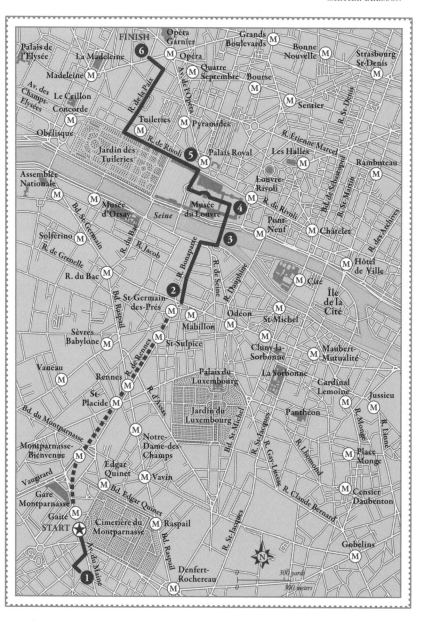

ℳ𝒶𝓅𝑜𝓁é𝑜𝓃 𝓑𝑜𝓃𝒶𝓅𝒶𝓇𝓉𝑒

"Even when I am gone, I shall remain in people's minds the star of their rights, my name will be the war cry of their efforts, the motto of their hopes."

Although many people have been shaped *by* Paris in one way or another, Napoléon Bonaparte is one of a select few who can claim to have actually shaped the city itself—quite literally. He had a megalomaniacal obsession with commemorating his numerous military victories with landmarks, which led to the construction of several of the city's most well-known monuments. It is thanks to him that we have the Arc de Triomphe, the Madeleine, the column at the Place Vendôme, and the Arc de Triomphe du Carrousel.

Napoléon was born on the island of Corsica in 1769. After attending military school, he joined the army and made his name fighting in conflicts in Italy and Egypt. He rose rapidly through the ranks until he initiated a coup d'état in 1799 and declared himself First Consul. By 1804, he'd pronounced himself emperor. A brilliant military strategist, he spent the better part of the next decade engaged in various battles with most of Europe—Austria, Britain, and Prussia—going to unprecedented lengths to secure more land for his empire.

To commemorate those who fought in the Revolutionary and Napoleonic wars, Napoléon initiated construction of the Arc de Triomphe. He had the column at the center of the Place Vendôme built as a tribute to the successful Battle of Austerlitz. Then he had the Église de la Madeleine completed as a temple to his Grande Armée (though this honor was later assumed by the Arc de Triomphe).

In addition to building monuments, Napoléon launched a program to modernize Paris. He wanted the city to reflect the glories of conquest and be worthy of his ever-expanding empire. To that end, he embarked on several ambitious construction projects, including the elegant arcades along the rue de Rivoli and the über-luxurious rue de la Paix (initially called rue Napoléon, of course). He also instituted practical urban improvements of the sewer and road systems.

More surprising, perhaps, was the legacy he left in the form of civilian reforms. He completely revamped the educational system, broadening its reach, centralizing control, and systematizing the curriculum. Though noble, it was all part of a grand plan to create more patriotic soldiers for his empire: "Of all our institutions,

public education is the most important. Everything depends on it, the present and the future. Above all we must secure unity: we must be able to cast a whole generation in the same mould." Finally, he instituted a set of civil laws dubbed the Napoleonic Code, many of which are still in place today.

He abdicated as emperor not once, but twice, falling from grace after the appalling losses his Grande Armée suffered in Russia in 1812, and then again after the unsuccessful battle of Waterloo. Following the latter, he was unceremoniously shipped off to the island of St. Helena, where he died several years later—a surprisingly lonely and undramatic ending for one of the most ambitious and influential figures in French history.

M: ÉCOLE MILITAIRE

Exit onto av. de la Motte-Picquet. You can't miss the **École Militaire** (1), whose grounds extend before you to the south. When Napoléon arrived in Paris at the age of fifteen, he attended military school here for a year. He emerged as an officer at the tender age of sixteen and joined the French army. Head up the avenue to the Hôtel des Invalides, which houses the sprawling **Musée de l'Armée** (2). In addition to numerous personal items (his uniforms, swords, telescopes, and epaulettes, the kind of military tent he slept in when out conquering foreign lands), you'll find a *very* thorough account of the emperor's many military triumphs (and few defeats). Captions appear in both French and English. At the southern end of the complex is the **Tombe de Napoléon** (3), a cavernous shrine to the man himself. At the center, beneath the dome, is the emperor's immense sarcophagus, inside of which are six nested coffins. On the lower level, you'll find engraved murals that describe his wide-ranging accomplishments, which extend far beyond his military triumphs. You'll find references to his commitment to education, industry, internal affairs, commerce, and more. Once you've had your fill, head north out of the Invalides across the esplanade, turn right at the quai and cross the Pont de la Concorde. Napoléon was responsible for launching the construction of the Arc de Triomphe, visible to the west as you cross the Place de la Concorde, as well as the **Église de la Madeleine** (4), straight up rue Royale. Although originally meant to serve as a temple honoring Napoléon's *Grande Armée*, la Madeleine was eventually consecrated as a church. Head east on the **rue de Rivoli** (5), which the emperor had built to commemorate his victory against Austria, at the battle of Rivoli. He specifically forbade the shops on this street to include anything practical or common (butchers, bakers, or "any other operation that requires an oven"). Look up rue de Castiglione. Napoléon was responsible for the column at the center of the **Place Vendôme** (6), which commemorates his victory at Austerlitz through a series of bronze plaques that spiral up the sides. Consider detouring up to the Palais Royal to enjoy lunch at the immaculately preserved **Grand Vefour** (7), where the emperor frequently dined with his wife, Josephine. Continue as far as Île de la Cité and cross onto the island to pay a visit to **Notre Dame** (8), where Napoléon was crowned emperor at the age of thirty-five in an immensely elaborate, three-plus-hour ceremony involving the Pope, virgin maidens, and diamond-encrusted coronation swords. Catch the metro at Cité.

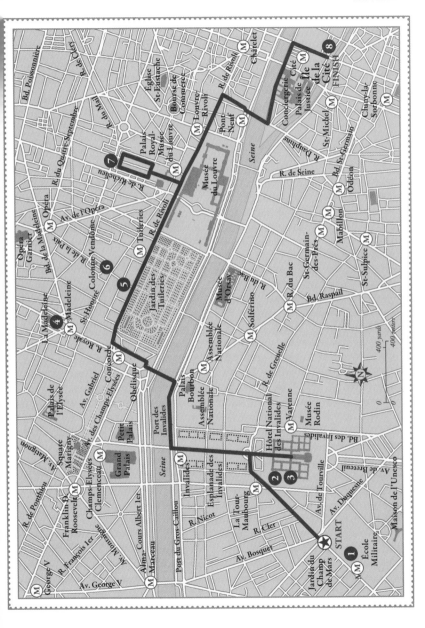

George Sand

"Whoever has loved knows all that life contains of sorrow and joy."

In an era when most women in France could aspire professionally to little more than being a seamstress or laundress, George Sand was enjoying enormous success as a writer, mingling with the luminaries of the age, and brazenly flouting convention—ruffled dresses? *Mais non!*—at every turn. George Sand was not only the most famous female writer in nineteenth-century France, but a wildly colorful and prodigiously energetic personality well ahead of her time.

Sand spent most of her youth on her family's estate in the countryside outside of Paris, then married a baron at the age of eighteen, and had two children. But she quickly grew restless and decided to pursue her own aspirations. Weary of the constraints of marriage, she negotiated a rather unusual deal with her husband that enabled her to spend part of each year writing in Paris. She arrived in the city in 1831. Within months, she had moved in with a younger lover and started writing for the newspaper *Le Figaro*. She cast off the corseted and fussy fashions of the era and took to dressing like a man, smoking cigars, and carousing in bars and cafés, claiming to love the anonymity and freedom that cross-dressing permitted her. Clearly, Paris suited her.

Her first novel, *Indiana*, catapulted her into the literary limelight, and she continued to write prodigiously for the rest of her life. Typically, Sand worked feverishly from midnight until dawn, pouring forth a steady stream of novels in the highly emotional Romantic style. Through her work, women's emotions and sexual desires were acknowledged for the first time in print, setting a provocative new precedent.

The public loved Sand's novels, but it was equally captivated by her life. Her writing may have focused on the romantic quest for love, but her own string of sensational romantic escapades was tempestuous, unpredictable, and an endless source of gossip. She dared to ask for a legal separation from her husband in an era when such an arrangement was unheard of. After her first lover, she moved on, going through a long list of young men. She had a stormy on-and-off-again affair with Romantic poet Alfred Musset, eventually running off with his doctor and leaving him ill in Venice. Her longest love affair was with the composer Frédéric Chopin. They were together for nine years, but even then she flouted convention, living in a separate apartment next door to him for most of that time.

For Sand, Paris meant liberation. Though many Parisians may not have known quite what to make of her—and plenty expressed outright disapproval—Paris changed everything for her: She found her true self, tapped into her creative talents, and enjoyed recognition for her work. In Paris, she had the opportunity to befriend intellectual equals; she found stimulation in literary salons; and, perhaps most important of all to her, she staved off boredom. Although she returned to the countryside in later life, Paris was the match that allowed her to light up the literary world for much of the nineteenth century.

M: St-Michel + metro ride to St-Georges

Head east down the quai to **29 quai St-Michel** (1) to view the building where the author lived with her first (and much younger) lover, Jules Sandeau, in an apartment from which he could easily escape if her husband showed up unannounced. Then backtrack and head west along the Seine. The beautifully preserved **Laperouse** (2; 51 quai des Grands Augustins) was one of Sand's favorite places to dine. It's worth splurging on a drink in the downstairs bar to enjoy the intimate gilded interior. Imagine the likes of Victor Hugo and Sand holding court at one of the tables upstairs. Turn left on rue Guénégaud, then right on rue Jacques Callot, and right on rue de Seine. This is where Sand stayed when she first arrived in Paris, moving into an apartment at #31 (3), also with Sandeau. Continue north and turn left on quai Malaquais. Sand lived at #19 (4) from 1832 to 1836; here, she hosted the luminaries of the age, including her new lover, Romantic poet Alfred Musset. Backtrack and head down rue Bonaparte. Turn left on rue Jacob and right on rue de Furstemberg to reach the **Musée Delacroix** (5). The Romantic painter Eugène Delacroix was one of Sand's closest friends, and she undoubtedly spent a good deal of time here since this was the artist's home and studio. Today, you'll find his paintings and personal effects, including a caricature of Sand. It's easy to imagine the friends deciding to treat themselves to dinner nearby at Laperouse or La Tour d'Argent (15 quai Tournelle), another favorite. Turn right on rue de l'Abbaye, turn left and cross through the square, and right on bd. St-Germain.

Take the metro from rue du Bac to St-Georges in La Nouvelle Athènes, a popular literary enclave in the nineteenth century. Sand lived here for many years with Frédéric Chopin, first on rue Laffitte, and later, in separate apartments in the secluded **Square d'Orléans** (6). To reach it, head south on rue St-Georges, turn right on rue d'Aumale, then left on rue Taitbout. Enter the square via 80 rue Taitbout. Backtrack, turn left on rue d'Aumale, then right on rue de la Rochefoucauld. Veer left on rue Fontaine, then turn left on rue Chaptal to reach the **Musée de la Vie Romantique** (7; 16 rue Chaptal). This small museum was home to Ary Scheffer, Sand's close friend, who held regular salons to which he invited the literati of the day. Today, the home is a tribute to Sand. You'll find several watercolors that she painted, portraits of the author and her children, and a Delacroix sketch of her country estate. Backtrack down rue Chaptal and continue along rue Notre-Dame-de-Lorette to return to the metro.

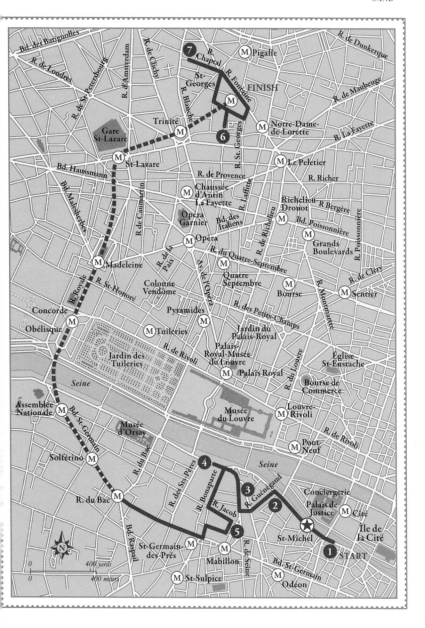

YVES SAINT LAURENT

"Fashions fade, style is eternal."

When Yves Saint Laurent arrived in Paris from Oran, Algeria, at the age of seventeen, he took the fashion world by storm. It wasn't long before he found himself working for Christian Dior, who saw a genius in the making and hired him on the spot. In 1955, when Dior died unexpectedly, Saint Laurent became the company's head designer at the tender age of twenty-one. Overnight, he was transformed into the darling of the world's fashion capital.

After several years at Dior, Saint Laurent ventured out on his own with the help of his companion and business partner, Pierre Bergé. From the moment the first models strutted down the runway in the new YSL designs, praise rained down on him from all sides. *Women's Wear Daily* declared him to be the "king of Paris." Almost twenty years later, he still reigned supreme. The *New York Times* said of his designs in 1976: "A revolutionary collection which will change the course of fashion in the world." And he continued to wield tremendous influence on the world of haute couture—and far beyond—for decades after.

It is perhaps difficult to comprehend just how revolutionary Saint Laurent and his designs were at the time. For Saint Laurent, fashion wasn't just about designing beautiful clothes (though that was certainly an important element). Fashion was an opportunity to make a statement. Saint Laurent's early, bold designs emerged during the '60s, when women were in the midst of a sexual revolution and were joining the workforce in ever-greater numbers. He understood that women wanted to project a new and more powerful image, and he gave them what they wanted. He famously designed the first pants suit for women, and, in a scandalous move, feminized the tuxedo, which had until then been the ultimate symbol of masculine style.

The designer adapted his fashions to current events in Paris (and beyond) in other ways, as well. He saw that the influence of haute couture was beginning to wane and that ready-to-wear fashions were the future. Wanting to make previously out-of-reach designs available to a wider audience, he was the very first haute couture designer to launch his own ready-to-wear line: Yves Saint Laurent Rive Gauche. In doing so, he made designer apparel more accessible to the mainstream while democratizing fashion in general, launching it in an entirely new

direction. With much of the world taking its fashion cues from Paris, it was the only place that Saint Laurent could ever have had such a profound effect on fashion—and on the way we dress today.

M: Alma-Marceau

Head up av. du Président Wilson, veer onto av. Marceau, and turn left on rue Léonce Reynaud to reach the one-time studio of Yves Saint Laurent at #3 (1). Today, it is open to the public as the Fondation Pierre Bergé–Yves Saint Laurent and hosts a few temporary, fashion-related exhibits per year, such as a retrospective on the tuxedo or a collection of Saint Laurent's designs. Backtrack and head up av. du Président Wilson to the **Palais Galliera** (2), home to the Musée de la Mode to see what's on display. When it's open, it too hosts a rotating lineup of fashion-focused exhibits. Retrace your steps and turn left on av. Montaigne, Paris's shrine to haute couture. The who's who of fashion all have boutiques along here, and the latest trends are debuted in the oversized windows. See if you can identify Saint Laurent's influence on today's clothing—women in pants suits? Check. Safariwear? Check. Trench coats? Check. Stop in for a drink at the sumptuous **Plaza Athénée** (3); Saint Laurent used to frequent the Relais Plaza restaurant within. If you're feeling peckish, **l'Avenue** (4; 41 av. Montaigne) is a stylish place to stop for a bite. Admire the new Saint Laurent flagship store at #53 (5). Cross the rond-point des Champs-Élysées onto av. Matignon and turn right on rue du Faubourg St-Honoré, which becomes rue St-Honoré. Check out what's new at **Yves Saint Laurent's Rive Gauche boutique** (6; 32–38 rue du Faubourg-St-Honoré). If you're curious where the city's real trendsetters are, pop into the chic **Hôtel Costes** (7; 239 rue St-Honoré), whose labyrinthine lobby and bar serve as ground zero for those in town for Fashion Week. Continue down rue St-Honoré and turn left into the Palais Royal to visit vintage collector **Didier Ludot** (8; 20–24 gal. de Montpensier and 125 gal. de Valois). Catch the metro at Palais Royal–Musée du Louvre.

Those curious to see where the designer lived should head south through the Tuileries, cross the Pont Royal, turn right on the quai, then left on rue de Bellechasse. Turn right on rue de Babylone to reach the building where Saint Laurent lived with his partner (both in business and life), Pierre Bergé, in sumptuous splendor at #77. Backtrack along rue de Babylone to wrap up your walk with a stroll through temple of style Au Bon Marché (24 rue de Sèvres). Catch the metro at Sèvres-Babylone.

Bonus: Saint Laurent loved Paris nightlife. Enjoy a night out at one of his favorite haunts after dark. Start with dinner at the Escargot Montorgueil (38 rue Montorgueil), where groups can book the designer's former table. Then head to swank nightclub Le Régine (49 rue de Ponthieu).

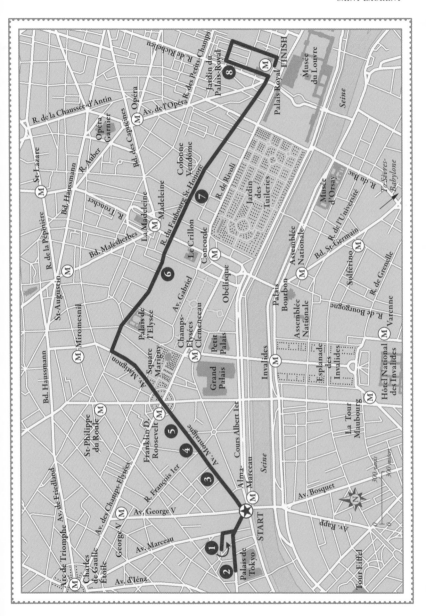

AUDREY HEPBURN

"Paris is always a good idea."
—FROM SABRINA

Audrey Hepburn may never have lived in Paris, but thanks to the many movies she filmed on location there, she will forever be linked with the City of Light. In her movies, Paris isn't just a backdrop but is often a central character; the films simply wouldn't have worked anywhere else.

The most obvious example of the city's star power is in *Sabrina,* in which Paris actually plays a pivotal role (even though none of the movie was actually filmed there). Sabrina goes off to Paris a provincial young girl and returns a woman of the world. She exclaims to Linus, "Paris isn't for changing planes, it's for changing your outlook! For throwing open the windows and letting in . . . letting in *la vie en rose*." Edith Piaf's signature song winds its way through the movie.

Sabrina also marked the beginning of Hepburn's enduring relationship with legendary French designer Hubert de Givenchy, who in the 1950s was still a rising star. Rumor has it that when they met, he was expecting Katharine Hepburn to walk through the door, not Audrey. But she won him over, and it was the start of a lifelong friendship. Givenchy went on to design many of Hepburn's costumes for later films. Givenchy couldn't have asked for a more elegant model for his designs, and he was deluged with clients after *Sabrina* came out. Hepburn, in turn, benefited from having the designer help her develop her signature style.

In *Love in the Afternoon*, a youthful Hepburn takes up with Gary Cooper, their liaison centered in a Ritz hotel room that overlooks the Place Vendôme. She's again wearing Givenchy (perhaps a bit of a stretch since she's playing an impoverished student).

In the thriller *Charade*, Hepburn runs—sometimes literally—all over Paris until she lands in the arms of Cary Grant. The director took them both out for dinner before filming started, and Hepburn was so nervous about meeting Grant for the first time that she spilled a glass of red wine down his suit. The incident was later incorporated into the film (but with ice cream instead of wine).

Paris-set *Funny Face* is known to be Audrey Hepburn's favorite film. An ode to fashion, a tribute to the city, and an enduring classic, this movie juxtaposed two contrasting worlds in Paris: the black turtleneck–wearing intellectual circle (the "Empathicalists") and the glittering world of haute couture. Rain

drenched Paris for weeks during the filming, but Hepburn probably didn't notice; she was fulfilling her childhood dream of dancing with Fred Astaire.

Paris When It Sizzles was not a success, and is considered one of the few missteps in Hepburn's illustrious career. Although it features scenes set at the Eiffel Tower and around the Champs-Élysées, it fizzled, rather than sizzled.

Even without a permanent address in Paris, Hepburn and the city will always share a strong association, as much to do with their shared grace and style as with the films she worked on there.

M: KLÉBER

Exit onto av. Kléber and cross the street to the discreet but sumptuous **Hôtel Raphael** (**1**; 17 av. Kléber), where Hepburn started each day when she was in Paris. It was her favorite hotel, and she was known for redecorating her suite completely with her own furnishings down to the last detail in order to create a sense of home while she was filming here. Head up to the Arc de Triomphe (one of the sites featured in *Funny Face*) and descend the Champs-Élysées. Turn left on av. Matignon. To the right is the garden where the **puppet theater** (**2**) in *Charade* is located. It still operates today (Wednesdays, Saturdays, Sundays at 3, 4, and 5 P.M.). Just beyond it, along av. Gabriel, is what remains of the **Marché aux Timbres** (**3**), which plays a key role in the film. Continue through the gardens. Just beyond the Théâtre Marigny, head south on av. W. Churchill to the **Pont Alexandre III** (**4**), Paris's most elaborate bridge, also featured in *Funny Face*. Retrace your steps and head down the allée Marcel Proust past the **U.S. Embassy** (**5**), another important location in *Charade*. Turn up rue Boissy d'Anglas and turn left on rue du Faubourg-St-Honoré to pay homage to the actress at **Givenchy** (**6**; 28 rue du Fbg. St-Honoré). This isn't the couturier's studio where Hepburn first met Hubert de Givenchy, but it's a convenient place to remember Audrey's classic style and the extraordinarily successful relationship that she enjoyed with the designer. Backtrack, and continue down the street, peeking up rue Castiglione to the **Place Vendôme** (**7**). Hepburn filmed *Love in the Afternoon* with Gary Cooper at the Ritz located on this square. Head south on rue Castiglione and turn left on rue de Rivoli. Stop for a *chocolat chaud* at **Angelina** (**8**; 226 rue de Rivoli), one of Hepburn's favorite spots, and still an immensely popular *salon de thé*. As you sip your hot chocolate in this timelessly elegant setting, consider Hepburn's line about Paris's influence in *Sabrina*: "I have learned how to live; how to be *in* the world and *of* the world. . . ." Cross into the Tuileries and stroll up to the Petit Carrousel, where Hepburn so charmingly releases the balloons in *Funny Face*. Beyond it is the Louvre; Hepburn's descent down the steps in front of *The Winged Victory of Samothrace* in her red dress, calling out to Fred Astaire, "Take the picture!" is one of the most iconic moments in film. Head north out of the gardens and cross into the **Palais Royal** (**9**), site of the famous, nail-biting chase at the end of *Charade*. Catch the metro at Palais Royal–Musée du Louvre.

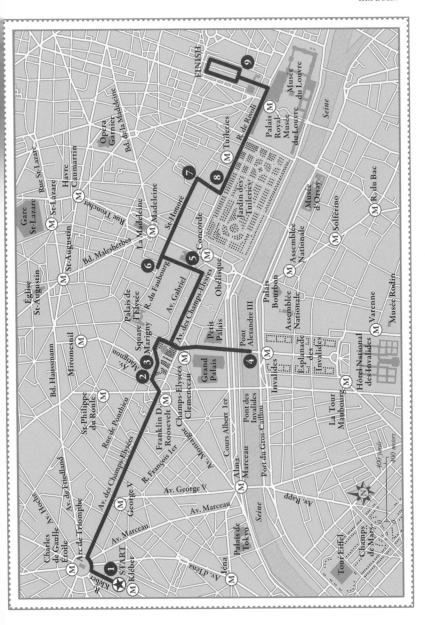

Victor Hugo

*"An invasion of armies can be resisted, but not
an idea whose time has come."*

Victor Hugo was more than just a writer. He was a poet, a politician, a novelist, a pioneer of the Romantic style, and a self-appointed ambassador for the poor and disenfranchised. He leapt to fame at an early age—earning a royal salary for his poetry by the age of twenty—and throughout his life, he used that power to bring attention to the misfortunes of others.

Born in the town of Besançon in 1802, Victor Hugo began writing as a child and was still just a teenager when he received his first accolades from the prestigious Académie Française for two poems he had submitted. By the age of thirty, with the publication of *The Hunchback of Notre Dame*, he'd become one of the country's most admired writers. Not one to rest on his laurels, he continued to write prolifically, and also ventured into politics. Initially a monarchist, he switched sides, eventually becoming a vocal promoter of human rights and the poor. In fact, when Napoléon III took over the government in a coup d'état, Hugo, having vilified the new leader, went into self-imposed exile for the following twenty years, living in Belgium and the Channel Islands for most of that time.

In 1862, while Hugo was still in exile, he published *Les Misérables*. Hugo's sprawling novel is an emotional powerhouse, exposing the sordid underbelly of Paris and the struggles of its inhabitants in haunting detail. The city of Paris itself is a central and defining character in his magnum opus. On the day it came out, bookstores were mobbed, and thousands of copies sold out in a single day. His books gave voice to a population that rarely had any, and he became the embodiment of hope for millions.

Indelibly shaped by the city he inhabited, Hugo in turn made a significant mark on Paris. We have *The Hunchback of Notre Dame* to thank for the fact that the legendary cathedral is still with us today. Hugo's novel about Quasimodo and Esmeralda inspired renewed interest in the landmark, which led to its being restored. (In fact, this renovation sparked a new appreciation for Gothic architecture across the country and led to the preservation of many of France's Gothic buildings.)

Later in his life, when he finally returned to his beloved city after his exile, he was elected to the Senate and

continued to champion the cause of the poor through politics and writing. An unprecedented two million people turned out for Hugo's funeral procession in 1885, which began at the Arc de Triomphe and led across the city to his final resting place at the Panthéon.

M: Bastille

Exit the place de la Bastille via rue St-Antoine and turn right on rue de Biragues. Enter the Place des Vosges and turn right beneath the arcades to reach the **Musée Victor Hugo (1)**, located in the square's southeast corner. Hugo lived on the third floor (2e étage) with his wife and four children for eighteen years before his exile. It was here that he wrote the notes for what would one day become *Les Misérables*. The museum not only contains interesting artifacts, but also displays the author's living spaces, complete with beautifully paneled rooms, a recreation of his elaborate *Salon Chinois*, his bedroom with his own bed, and an imposing sculpture of the author by Rodin. Exit the square the way you entered, turn right on rue St-Antoine, then left on rue du Pont Louis-Philippe. Cross the Île St-Louis onto Île de la Cité, then turn right onto rue du Cloître Notre-Dame, passing the Café Esmerelda (named after one of the characters in Hugo's *The Hunchback of Notre-Dame*). **Notre Dame (2)** rises before you. In desperate need of repair back in Hugo's day, it was in danger of being demolished until the book appeared. Today, after a thorough cleaning, it's looking more splendid than ever. Fans of the book should follow in the steps of Quasimodo and Esmerelda and climb the towers—you'll be amply rewarded for your efforts with lovely views. Interestingly, many of the iconic gargoyles weren't added until the restoration, fueled by the novel's popularity. Descend and cross over to the Left Bank. Turn right on the quai to reach **Laperouse (3;** 51 quai des Grands Augustins), where Hugo frequently dined. It remains one of Paris's most romantic and beautifully preserved restaurants. (If you're not up for a full meal here, enjoy a drink in the intimate ground-floor bar.) Head down rue Dauphine, veer right onto rue de Buci, then turn right on bd. St-Germain. As you admire the **Cathedral St-Germain-des-Prés (4)** on your right (the oldest cathedral in Paris), give thanks once again to Hugo, who led the restoration effort. Continue down bd. St-Germain to the **Musée des Lettres et Manuscrits (5;** 222, bd. St-Germain). A handwritten letter that Hugo wrote to George Sand and several poems and manuscript pages penned by Hugo do a good job of bringing the legend to life. Catch the metro at Solférino.

Bonus: Backtrack down the boulevard and turn right on rue de Seine, which becomes rue de Tournon. Cross into the Luxembourg Gardens and exit out the east side onto rue Soufflot to reach the Panthéon, where Hugo is buried.

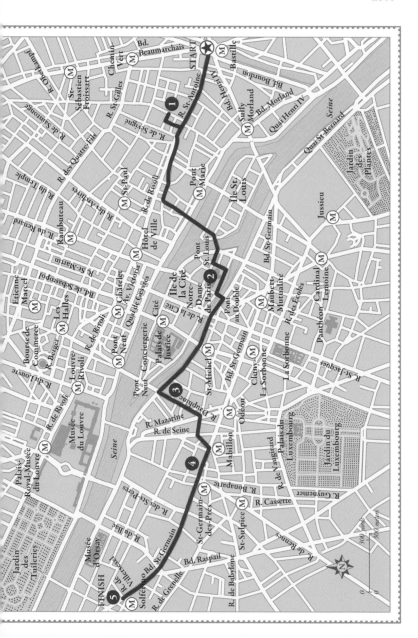

MARIE ANTOINETTE

*"Courage! I have shown it for years;
think you I shall lose it at the
moment when my sufferings are to end?"*

Marie Antoinette was born in Vienna in 1755. Forced into an arranged marriage to cement a strategic alliance between Austria and France, the young girl left her beloved homeland and family at fourteen and was handed off to the French in a stupendously elaborate ritual on an island in the middle of the Rhine, which separated the two countries. There, she shed all of her Austrian garments and stepped into France in French clothing. When she finally arrived at Versailles, she married Louis XVI, the future king.

By the age of nineteen, Marie Antoinette was the queen of France. Although she found herself at the head of a prestigious and influential empire, she chaffed at the constricting formality of life at Versailles. Many of her daily rituals—dining and even getting dressed—were open to select members of the public. Even on her wedding night, an audience was permitted to watch as the two young royals were helped into their nightclothes and climbed into bed. She could not so much as pick up a garment, but had to wait for it to be handed to her by the highest-ranking person in the room.

To make matters worse, the king had no interest in consummating their marriage, and their (lack of) sex life was a topic of endless fascination to the public. Ultimately, it was she who bore the public burden of his lack of interest. Tension grew as the public awaited the birth of what they assumed would be the future king, and the queen was increasingly ostracized for her inability to deliver a child. Seven years after they married, Marie Antoinette finally gave birth to a daughter, and eventually had three more children, including the long-awaited dauphin (who would not, as it turned out, ever become the king of France).

Bored, far from home, weighed down by a never-ending series of royal obligations, and married to someone she didn't love, the young queen sought to divert herself with increasingly frivolous distractions. She spent lavishly on new fashions, took to gambling, threw extravagant parties, and extensively renovated the Petit Trianon, a villa on the grounds of Versailles that the king had given to her. In another era, this decadence might have gone unnoticed, but in the late 1700s, many people in France were starving and still more were

fed up with the increasing excesses of the monarchy. Unwittingly, Marie Antoinette became the embodiment of the frivolity and self-indulgence of the Old Regime. As the French Revolution took hold, the public turned its full wrath upon her, tracking down the royal family as they attempted to escape, and imprisoning them in Paris. On the day of her execution, at the age of thirty-seven, the former queen was transported in an open-air carriage (the better to allow people to scorn her) from the Conciergerie to what is now the Place de la Concorde. Alternately pitied as an unfortunate young girl thrust into an impossible role and reviled as a self-indulgent dilettante, Marie Antoinette continues to captivate centuries after she made her mark on Paris and the world.

RER C: to Versailles Rive Gauche*

Start your tour with a visit to the interior of the **Petit Trianon** (**1**). Originally built by Louis XV for his mistress Madame de Pompadour, the villa was later a gift from Louis XVI to his young queen. Weary of the stifling formality of the palace, Marie Antoinette wasted no time transforming the Petit Trianon into her personal sanctuary. Her bedroom, with its sunny floral fabrics and chairs carved with vines and upholstered with cornflowers (her favorite flower) are all a far cry from the gilded Rococo splendor of the palace. Venture outside into the Domaine. The queen had an entire formal French garden razed here and replaced it with a more natural-looking English-style garden. Loop around the pond, stopping at the **Théâtre de la Reine** (**2**). She performed for a select group of friends here, even going so far as to act in *The Marriage of Figaro*, which the king had previously forbidden to be staged. Stroll down to **La Ferme** (**3**). Although it's a real working farm today, complete with goats and honking geese, the buildings look much as they did when Marie Antoinette ordered them built: like part of a stage set. Continue on to the rustic **Hameau de la Reine** (**4**), where Marie Antoinette used to play at being a simple milkmaid (she didn't actually do any of the work, but liked to dress the part). Meander back via the **Temple de l'Amour** (**5**). Loop around to the formal **French garden** (**6**). With its straight lines and closely clipped shrubbery, it stands in marked contrast to the romantic Domaine. Continue through the garden to the **Grand Trianon** (**7**). Although the queen didn't care for it, the pink-marble building, with its views and extensive gardens, is worth the detour.

Back in Paris, you can extend your tour by visiting the Conciergerie (bd. du Palais, Île de la Cité), where Marie Antoinette was imprisoned for her final weeks. Her cell has been reconstructed to look as though she is still there (complete with a black-cloaked mannequin). The Musée Carnavelet (23 rue de Sevigné), the national French history museum, displays paintings that depict the former queen being separated from her family, and also holds some of her personal effects.

(Purchase a ticket valid for zones 1–4.) Note that not all C trains go to Versailles. Be sure to catch a C5 train. To reach the Domaine, walk the half mile to the main palace. Either walk from the palace through the gardens (just over a mile), rent bicycles at the Grand Canal, or take the mini-train from the north terrace of the palace. The Petit Trianon does not open until noon.

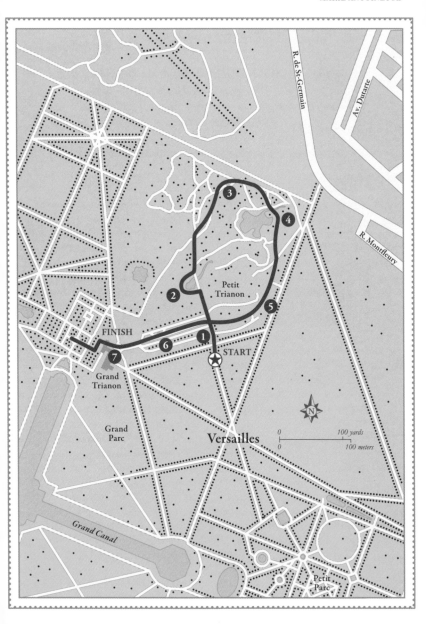

HENRY MILLER & ANAÏS NIN

"Certainly I . . . starved in Paris but it was different. I was a romantic beggar, so to speak. I starved in great company. My predecessors were, or became, illustrious figures."
— HENRY MILLER

"We write to taste life twice, in the moment and in retrospect."
—ANAÏS NIN

Henry Miller and Anaïs Nin spent only a few years together in Paris, but they will forever be associated with the city that brought them together.

Anaïs Nin was born right outside of Paris in Neuilly in 1903. She spent most of her childhood in New York and only returned to Paris in 1924, as a newlywed, when her husband, Hugh Parker Guiler, was assigned to a bank position there. At first, she didn't particularly care for the city, but then she and her husband joined the thriving avant-garde scene and she met the man who would change her life: Henry Miller.

Miller was born in New York and arrived in Paris with just a few cents in his pocket. He found its heady intellectual atmosphere and freedoms intoxicating, and he wandered the streets day and night, steeping himself in the life of the city. The cafés became his lifeblood, and he spent his days observing and writing for hours on end. As Nin later said, "He talks with everybody, his café life, his conversations with people in the street, which I once considered an interruption to writing, I now believe to be a quality which distinguishes him from other writers." Paris unlocked Miller's untapped creative reserves, and he used those early experiences in the city as fodder for his first book, *Tropic of Cancer.*

Miller and Nin met in 1931, and what started out as a literary friendship rapidly spiraled into a famously passionate love affair. Miller awakened Nin's senses, shook her out of a sort of spiritual torpor, and gave her a new perspective on Paris. No longer sidelined in the suburbs, she became a mainstay of the avant-garde, soaking up everything new and fresh and modern as she mingled with the literati and artists of Montparnasse. Having shunned Paris, she now embraced it: "It is Henry who is dispelling the fogs of shyness, of solitude, taking me through the street, and keeping me in a café—until dawn." She continues, "When I walk around Paris, I see and

sense much more than I did before, my eyes have been opened by Henry's revelations."

Miller's explosive *Tropic of Cancer* was published in Europe in 1934 (thanks to Nin, who paid for it to be printed). Although it only came out in the United States in 1961 (after censorship laws were changed), it nevertheless succeeded in launching Miller's career as a writer. Nin's

writing about this period wasn't published until decades later, but her diaries about her time in Paris—and her love affair depicted in erotic detail—belatedly catapulted her into the limelight.

With war looming, Miller and Nin parted ways, left Paris, and returned to the States in 1939. Nin went to New York with Hugh, while Miller moved to California.

M: Alésia

You'll emerge from the metro at a massive intersection. As you look around, keep in mind that a tour of Nin and Miller's stomping grounds doesn't offer many typically picturesque glimpses of Paris, but given their interests, this is entirely appropriate. Miller drew his inspiration and material from the city's seedy underbelly, not the sparkling *quais* of the Seine. This is the Paris that transformed him into a writer—and gave Nin her voice. Two of Miller's favorite cafés are right here. The **Bouquet d'Alésia** (**1**; 75 av. du Général Leclerc) is open until 4 A.M. Beneath a yellow awning is the **Brasserie Zeyer** (**2**; 62 rue d'Alésia), an atmospheric spot with potted palms and historic pictures of the neighborhood. Miller explains, "Hardly a day of my life, after moving to the Villa Seurat, ever passed without a drink or two at either Café Zeyer or the Café Bouquet d'Alésia." Head east on rue d'Alésia, turn right on rue de la Tombe-Issoire, then left on the tiny, quiet Villa Seurat. Miller lived on the top floor at #14 (**3**) from 1934 to 1939 when *Tropic of Cancer* came out. Backtrack and turn right, then left back onto rue d'Alésia, and right on av. du Général Leclerc. Turn left on rue Froidevaux and right on rue Schoelcher. Nin lived at #11bis (**4**)—also once home to Simone de Beauvoir—with her husband Hugh when they first moved to Paris. Backtrack and continue down rue Froidevaux, turn right on av. du Maine, then veer onto rue de la Gaîté. Lined with sex shops and x-rated video stores with names like L'Odyssex and New Sex Paradise, this was—perhaps unsurprisingly—one of Henry Miller's favorite streets. Imagine Miller here in the evenings, keenly observing the scene and gathering material for his next book. At rue du Maine, look left down the street and you'll see a sign for the **Hôtel Central** (**5**; 1 bis rue du Maine). This is where Miller and Nin began their steamy affair (in Room 40, if you must know). Continue straight, veering right up rue Delambre to reach the Carrefour Vavin, the hub of Montparnasse café life. Turn left to reach **Le Select** (**6**; 99 bd. du Montparnasse), or head to **La Rotonde** (**7**; #105), where Miller first confessed to Nin that he'd written her a love letter—but that he'd torn it up. At **Café du Dôme** (**8**; #108), you'll find photos of illustrious former customers lining the walls. Don't pass up the opportunity to sit in their company and watch the world go by. Catch the metro at Vavin.

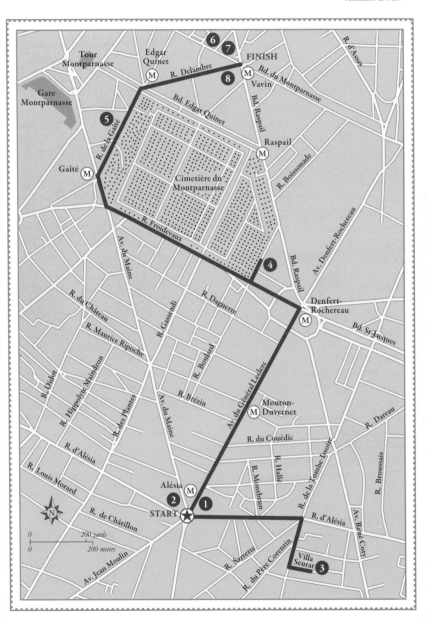

CLAUDE MONET

"I perhaps owe having become a painter to flowers."

With Monet's Impressionist paintings now a ubiquitous symbol of French artwork, it's almost impossible to grasp how radical his style appeared to the all-powerful art establishment of his time. Monet faced many years of scorn and derision and was repeatedly rejected from the major annual salon, but he remained true to his artistic beliefs—and, as we know, emerged triumphant in the end.

Even as a youth in the 1840s in Normandy, where he moved when he was five, Monet was drawn to art. He drew charcoal caricatures, which he sold on the street for a few *sous*. Finally, in 1859, he realized that if he wanted to pursue art seriously, he needed to go to Paris. His funds were limited, so he enrolled at the École Suisse, not far from the more prestigious École des Beaux Arts, and went to work studying the techniques of the Old Masters. As part of their training, the young art students set off to the Louvre just across the Seine to improve their skills by copying the great works within. Monet, however, wasn't interested in copying what had already been done. Instead, he set himself up by the windows, and, captivated by the movement of light on the sky and the river, he painted what he saw outside. Capturing

moments like this would remain a prominent theme in his work for the rest of his life.

This philosophy of painting did not lead to early success. Although Paris was the center of the art world, the establishment had very narrow and precise ideas about what talent looked like. Monet submitted his work to the annual Art Salon, only to see it rejected every time. Finally, in 1874, he and his friends set up their own independent salon. Although early critics were disparaging, the young artists persevered, gradually gaining a bigger following. For Monet, Paris served as a sort of anti-muse—having studied what the Parisian art world had to offer, he saw an opportunity to create something startling and new.

But the city did help him in one invaluable way: He found a like-minded group, who supported each other financially, provided inspiration and insight, encouraged each other's experimentation, and generally gave one another the confidence to carry on in the face of overwhelming criticism. Dubbed *Impressionists*, they were a tight bunch in the early years and gathered frequently in cafés in the place Pigalle. They shared studio space, painted the same subject matter, and,

of course, exhibited together for several years at the Salon Indépendant.

Monet was never, at heart, a Parisian, and he spent the last forty years of his life in Giverny. But it was in Paris that he made a name for himself and in Paris that he found an artistic community who supported him as he embarked on a rebellion that forever changed the course of art.

M: Notre-Dame-de-Lorette

Although we often associate Monet with Giverny, he spent his first few years here, a child of the city. The church at the exit to the metro station, **Notre-Dame-de-Lorette** (**1**), is where Monet was baptized, and he lived just down the street with his parents at **45 rue Laffitte** (**2**). Monet used to frequent the candy shop **Fouquet** (**3**; 36 rue Laffitte) just a few doors down. Head south on rue Laffitte and turn right on bd. des Italiens. Farther down this same boulevard at 35 bd. des Capucines, Monet and his friends (including Pissarro, Degas, Sisley, Renoir, and Cezanne) staged their first independent salon in 1874. The show was not an immediate success—critics thought the artwork appeared unfinished, and some even accused the painters of having subversive political motives. Turn left on rue de La Michodière to reach the restaurant **Drouant** (**4**; 18 rue Gaillon), which Monet frequented for Friday night suppers with friends. Continue south on rue Gaillon, turn left on rue des Petits-Champs, which becomes rue Étienne Marcel. Turn right on **rue Montorgueil** (**5**), the subject of one of Monet's rare urban paintings (picture it with a riot of French flags flapping in the breeze). Turn right on rue Rambuteau (which becomes rue Coquillière), then left on rue du Louvre. Jog right at rue de Rivoli to enter the **Cour Carrée du Louvre** (**6**). Monet used to come here to study the works of the masters, but he was more intrigued by the play of light on the water outside. Cross the Pont des Arts and head south on gallery-lined rue de Seine. Turn right to reach **#20 rue Visconti** (**7**), where Monet shared a studio with his friend Auguste Renoir in their early, impoverished days. Turn right on rue Bonaparte, heading past the École des Beaux-Arts, the hub of the artistic establishment. Turn left at the quai, then cross the Seine and head into the Tuileries to the **Musée de l'Orangerie** (**8**), home to Monet's *Les Nymphéas*. Eight murals of water lilies displayed in two luminous oval rooms envelop the viewer. You'll find more Impressionist works on the lower level. Catch the metro at Concorde.

Bonus: Anyone who loves Monet should not miss the Musée d'Orsay, famous for its collection of Impressionist works (a discounted ticket will gain you entry to both the Orangerie and the Musée d'Orsay). But the ultimate Monet showcase is the Musée Marmottan (2 rue Louis Boilly). Located on the western edge of the city, it houses the largest collection of Monet's work in the world, including *Impression, Sunrise,* which gave the movement its name.

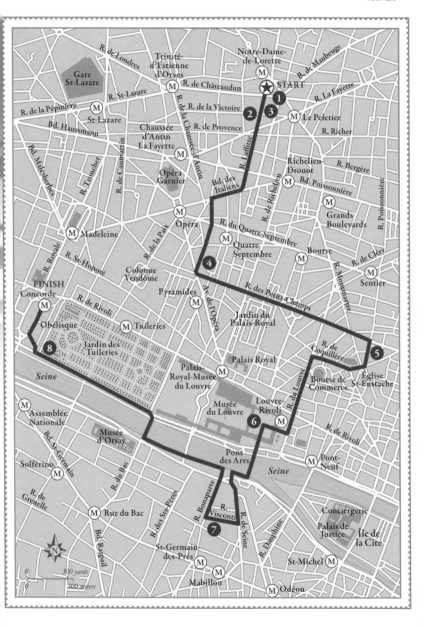

Serge Gainsbourg

*"There's a trilogy in my life, an equilateral triangle,
shall we say, of Gitanes, alcoholism and girls."*

Serge Gainsbourg was France's favorite bad boy. Controversial, scandalous, and fueled by an endless supply of booze and Gitanes cigarettes, he took Paris—and the world—by storm with his famous song "Je t'aime—moi non plus." The song was banned in several countries and denounced by the Vatican; the album even carried a sticker saying it was forbidden to those under the age of twenty-one. The torrent of publicity that resulted from all this controversy only helped fuel worldwide sales.

Gainsbourg's career got off to a bit of an erratic start. He was adrift in his early years, pursuing painting before setting his sights on music. This turning point came while he was watching Boris Vian perform—thereafter, Gainsbourg embraced songwriting with feverish intensity. He began to make a name for himself with "Le Poinçonneur des Lilas," about a metro-ticket controller.

From that point forward, Gainsbourg was heralded as one of France's greatest songwriters, and he stayed in the limelight, evolving his style to suit changing tastes and times, from jazz to pop and rock to reggae to electronica. He is equally famous for his steamy love life and hard living. He had a passionate and well-publicized affair with French icon Brigitte Bardot, then spent thirteen years of his life with Jane Birkin, with whom he had a daughter, Charlotte, who became an acclaimed singer and actress in her own right. For years, he partied the night away in clubs all over Paris, endlessly smoking Gitanes, and sleeping by day.

Especially in his later years, Gainsbourg sought out opportunities to be provocative at every turn—and not just with his suggestive song lyrics. He caused an uproar when he burned a 500-franc note to protest higher taxes; he insulted other celebrities on television; and he revealed lurid details about his romantic affairs. Jane Birkin left him, distressed by his heavy drinking and his seemingly constant need for drama. He got involved with another young model, nicknamed Bamboo, and had a son with her. But he couldn't overcome his alcoholism and continued to thrive on scandal and insult. At one point, after doing a reggae version of the French national anthem *La Marseillaise*, in which he mangled some of the original lyrics (using "etc." rather than the original words), the French newspaper *Le Figaro* declared that he

should have his citizenship revoked. Later on, while touring France, he received bomb threats at concerts. The French public raptly followed stunt after stunt, each more outrageous than the last.

Gainsbourg's hard living finally caught up with him, and he died at the age of sixty-two in his home on rue de Verneuil in 1991. His home has been left exactly as it was when he died, tended by his daughter Charlotte.

M: Pigalle

Head east on bd. de Clichy and up rue des Martyrs to the red, graffiti-covered drag bar **Madame Arthur** (**1**; 75bis rue des Martyrs). This is where Serge Gainsbourg got his start playing the piano. Backtrack and head down rue Jean-Baptiste Pigalle; turn right on rue Chaptal to visit his former home at **#11** (**2**), where he lived with his older sister, his twin sister, and his parents. Continue straight, turn left on rue Blanche (where a young Gainsbourg attended school as a child) to Trinité, where he used to play ball. Continue south on rue Mogador, veer right on rue Scribe, turn left on rue Daunou and right on rue de la Paix (which turns into place Vendôme) to reach the **Ritz** (**3**). The Hemingway Bar within (open from 6:30 P.M. to 2 A.M.) was one of the songwriter's favorite watering holes. Despite his provocative nature, he gravitated to places like this: private, intimate, quiet, and utterly deluxe. In fact, for all that he projected himself as a rebel in his music, he lived in some of the city's most posh neighborhoods and frequented its most staid bars. Continue down to rue de Rivoli, cross through the Tuileries to the Louvre's Cour Carrée; turn right and cross the Pont des Arts. Head south on rue Bonaparte. Turn left onto rue des Beaux Arts to peek into the discreet but luxurious **L'Hôtel** (**4**; 13 rue des Beaux Arts). Gainsbourg and Jane Birkin spent their first year as a couple here. She was just twenty-two to his forty-one, and it was the start of a passionate and highly public romance. They soon became the darlings of Paris, easily recognizable on their tandem bike by day and highly visible in the club scene by night. Backtrack and continue south on rue Bonaparte. Turn right on rue Jacob, right on rue des Sts-Pères, and left onto rue de Verneuil. It's hard to miss Gainsbourg's one-time home: It's the one covered in graffiti at **#5bis** (**5**). He lived here from 1969 until his death in 1991. Although it measured less than 900 square feet, he referred to it as his *hôtel particulier* (his mansion). He had the walls painted black, and filled the apartment with eclectic works of art. Continue straight and turn left on rue du Bac to reach the metro.

Diehard fans can continue their pilgrimage at the secluded Hôtel Raphael (17 av. Kleber, 16th arr.) near the Arc de Triomphe, another luxurious haven where Gainsbourg ensconced himself for long periods. Have a drink in his honor, then check out Le Raspoutine (58 rue de Bassano, 8th arr.), a classic bar he frequented in the '80s; he brought Birkin here for their first date.

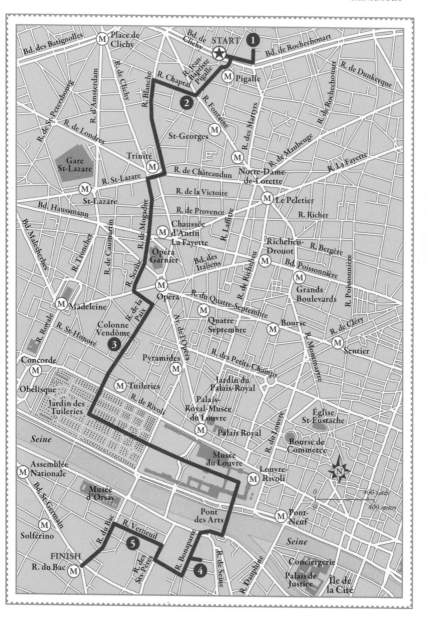

ℋENRI ℳATISSE

"An artist is an explorer."

When Matisse's *Woman with a Hat* was first exhibited at the annual Paris Salon in 1905, people were so outraged by the painting that they clawed at it with their fingernails. Matisse and his fellow painters were dubbed the "Fauves" (wild beasts), and Matisse was, for better or worse, crowned as their ringleader. The public didn't know it yet, but his painting had just created a seismic shift within the art world. One of the masters of Modernism had just made his first mark.

The young Matisse had intended to go into the field of law, but he contracted appendicitis when he was twenty-one and ended up bedridden. To distract him during his convalescence, his mother bought him some art supplies—and changed the course of his life. He later explained, "From the moment I held the box of colors in my hands, I knew this was my life. I threw myself into it like a beast that plunges toward the thing it loves."

He set off for Paris in 1891, where he lived off half-rations in primitive garrets, determined to stretch his meager resources long enough to establish himself. Although he started out copying the Old Masters, he became increasingly eager to break with the established artistic traditions. He grew bolder and began to experiment with color, for which he was widely criticized.

Among the few who spotted his early genius were the Steins—Gertrude and her brother Leo. They purchased the controversial *Woman with a Hat* and went on to befriend the artist. Gertrude's sister-in-law Sarah Stein became Matisse's biggest supporter. She publicized, validated, and encouraged him in his early years, when the public expressed nothing but contempt for him.

Fatefully, at one of Gertrude Stein's famous Saturday evening salons, Matisse met Pablo Picasso. From that point forward, they would be lifelong friends and rivals. Although they had wildly divergent styles—and were of quite different temperaments—each considered the other to be the only other artist worthy of his respect. They parlayed their rivalry into a productive relationship, spurring each other on even as they pursued different paths to greatness. Picasso later said, "No one has ever looked at Matisse's paintings more carefully than I; and no one has looked at mine more carefully than he."

Matisse found much of his artistic inspiration in the sunshine and bright colors of the south of France,

returning there again and again, but Paris was crucial to his professional development. It was in Paris that he enjoyed the support and encouragement of the Steins, rubbed shoulders with other artists, and had a chance to influence other emerging talents. Without Paris, it would have been virtually impossible for him to gain the kind of name recognition and global influence that he attained. He returned to Paris on and off for the rest of his life, but in 1917 he settled permanently in the brightly lit Mediterranean, and lived in Nice until he died in 1954.

101

M: Gaîté

Head north on av. du Maine and turn right onto rue du Maine, where Matisse lived in a very plain building at #12 (1) in his early, impoverished years. Back then, the building was so far off the beaten path that it stood surrounded by fields and pastures, and Matisse subsisted mostly on his massive artistic ambition. Turn left on rue de la Gaîté and continue up rue Delambre to bd. du Montparnasse. Although he was to become one of the most celebrated artists in the world and occasionally spent time with Picasso in the neighborhood's famous cafés, Matisse spent little time mingling with the other artists, preferring to devote himself completely to his work. Head north along bd. Raspail. Turn right on rue de Fleurus, where Gertrude Stein lived at #27 (you'll also pass the Café Constant at 37 rue d'Assas, which serves one of the richest cups of hot chocolate in Paris). Stein and Matisse became good friends, and she purchased many of his paintings over the years. She was also responsible for first introducing Matisse to his future friend and rival, Pablo Picasso. Turn left onto rue Madame. Sarah Stein, Gertrude's sister-in-law, lived at #58 (2), and she took an even greater interest in Matisse than Gertrude did, going to great lengths to give his artwork greater exposure and prominence. At one point, she had twelve of his paintings up on a single wall in her apartment on rue Madame.

Continue onto rue du Sabot then left on rue du Four and right on rue du Dragon. Matisse took his first art classes at the **Académie Julien** (3; 31 rue du Dragon). Continue north and turn right on bd. St-Germain. Turn left up rue de l'Ancienne Comédie and stop at **Café Procope** (4; #13), where Matisse mingled with fellow art students in his early days. Continue straight and turn right on rue St-André des Arts. Turn left on bd. St-Michel and right at the quai to view the building that Matisse inhabited (5; #19) twice, in different apartments. Though primitive, this is where he had his first private studio, a personal milestone. He painted the views of the Seine from his window here. Head north across the Petit Pont up rue St-Martin to the **Centre Pompidou** (6), where you'll find an impressive selection of Matisse's works, including his iconic gouache cutouts. It's worth the trip to see his magnificent *Polynesia, the Sea*. Catch the metro at Rambuteau.

Bonus: Note that you'll find other examples of Matisse's work at the Musée d'Art Moderne de la Ville de Paris (11 av. du President Wilson, 16th arr.), including *The Unfinished Dance* and *The Dance of Paris* (and a wonderful collection of Fauve art).

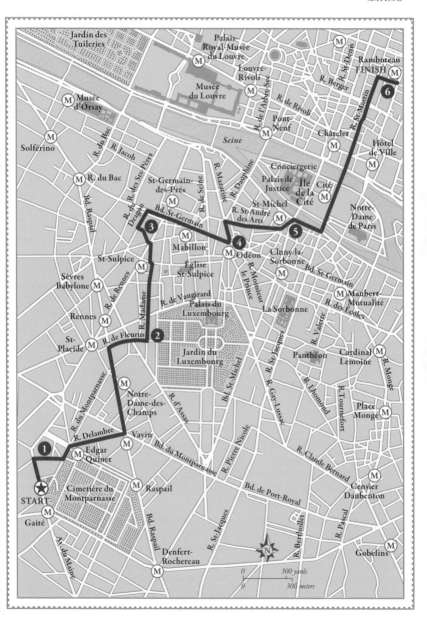

COLETTE

"I love my past, I love my present. I am not ashamed of what I have had, and I am not sad because I no longer have it."

In 1893, at the age of twenty, Colette arrived in Paris as a naïve young country girl on the arm of her new husband. Already a well-known cad, Henri Gauthier-Villars, better known as Willy, made his money through ghostwriters and kept mistresses on the side from the start. It wasn't long before he put Colette to work writing for him, too (which may have been the only positive influence he had on her life). *Claudine at School*, loosely based on Colette's own life story, was an instant bestseller when it came out, sparking a merchandising craze that included perfume and cigarettes named after the title character. Several other books in the Claudine series followed. Though this success should have marked the beginning of fame and fortune for Colette, Willy had the audacity to take sole credit for the books.

In 1906, Colette had endured enough of Willy's ways and moved out. She finally claimed authorship of the Claudine series (though Willy continued to rake in the royalties from the first books) and embarked on an affair of her own with the Marquise de Balbeuf, a wealthy lesbian known as Missy. Their liaison marked the first of many scandals that would feature the ever-sensual Colette during her life. She was soon performing at the Moulin Rouge, famously causing a riot when she locked lips with Missy on stage. Other affairs followed. Colette went on to remarry twice more, at one point seducing her sixteen-year-old stepson. Despite her tumultuous personal life, she still found time to write, often choosing to focus on unconventional relationships. She published her famous *Cheri*, about an aging courtesan's affair with a much younger man, in 1920. Eventually, Colette settled in an apartment in the Palais Royal with her third (much younger) husband. There, she wrote what is probably her best-known novel, *Gigi*, during the Nazi occupation of Paris during World War II, even as she kept her Jewish husband out of sight in their apartment.

Courting scandal, much beloved, and determined to live life on her own terms and to its fullest—others be damned—Colette was one of Paris's most devoted pupils. In Paris she grew up and discovered a bewildering complexity and variety of relationships. Paris taught her about love, sex, and power, all of which she then channeled into juicy fodder for her

novels. Although tales of her own sexual escapades sometimes eclipse her writing, she is still considered to be one of France's greatest writers. She was both a member, and, for a time, president of the prestigious Académie Goncourt and a member of the Legion of Honor. By the end of her life, she had written some fifty novels, a number of which were turned into plays and films. She continued to live at the Palais Royal until her death in 1954, a beloved Parisian fixture who could sometimes be spotted in her window, surrounded by cats and observing passersby.

M: Courcelles

Head north to **93 rue de Courcelles** (**1**) to view where Colette moved in 1896 with the infamous Willy. With the publication of the Claudine books, they were moving up in the world and could afford to leave the less-chic Left Bank behind. (As Claudine's Aunt Coeur muses, "wouldn't you rather have a pretty, light flat like this than be on that dirty Left Bank where no nice people live?") They moved up the street to 177bis rue de Courcelles in 1902. Colette had a trapeze and parallel bars installed there so that she could train for her stage performances. Given the unconventional life she would lead later on, it's perhaps surprising that she ended up in this staid quarter, one of the city's staunchest bastions of tradition. Retrace your steps and turn left to enter the **Parc Monceau** (**2**) via the black-and-gold wrought-iron gates. Colette used to stroll here, and set a scene from *Claudine à Paris* within: "The green Parc Monceau, with its soft lawns veiled in misty curtains of spray from the sprinklers, attracted me, like something good to eat. . . . Those lawns are swept like floors!" Impeccably maintained and dotted with statuary, ponds, and gazebos, the park has changed little since Colette's day. A visit to the nearby **Musée Jacquemart-André** (**3**; 158 bd. Haussmann) offers a glimpse at the interior of one of the neighborhood's handsome buildings. Given her lifelong love of food, Colette would undoubtedly have approved of your taking a break for a treat at the timelessly elegant *salon de thé* within. Turn right on bd. Malesherbes. Colette spent time all over this neighborhood: At various points in her life, she could be found dancing at the legendary Folies Bergère, running her own cosmetics business on rue Miromesnil, or living large at Claridge's on the Champs-Élysées. Turn left on rue Chauveau-Lagarde. Head past the food shops near la Madeleine (where Colette was denied a state funeral because she was a divorcée) and continue straight. Turn left on rue Gaillon. Stop for lunch at **Drouant** (**4**; 18 rue Gaillon), a literary restaurant where Colette has a private room named after her. Backtrack and continue east on rue des Petits-Champs. Turn right on rue Vivienne. Colette lived at **9 rue de Beaujolais** (**5**) in the Palais Royal for the final sixteen years of her life—longer than anywhere else in Paris. You'll find a plaque in her honor. At the **Grand Vefour** (**6**) her favorite table is also identified with a plaque. Alternatively, consider backtracking to dine at **Maxim's** (**7**; 3 rue Royale), where Colette's character Gigi spends an evening with the handsome Gaston Lachaille. Catch the metro at Palais Royal–Musée du Louvre.

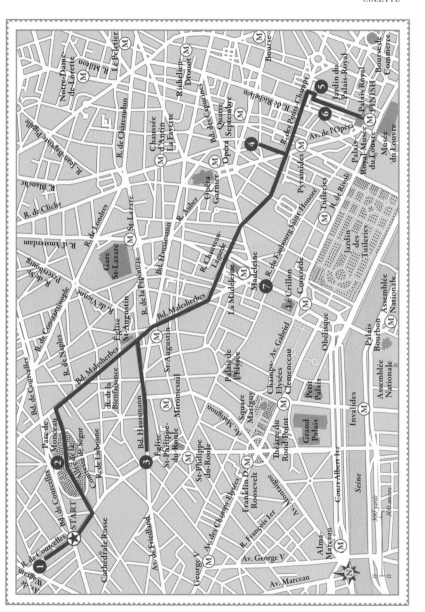

ACKNOWLEDGMENTS

An extraordinary number of people have helped me discover the city over the years. Long ago, my French grandmother exposed to me to the antidiluvian world of Parisian customs and etiquette, and my father revealed to me his childhood haunts. Over the years, my mother taught me how to shop in Paris, first for school supplies, later for earrings and scarves, and, eventually, for a wedding dress at Printemps. My brother rang in the millennium with me perched on a rooftop on rue Vital so that we could see the Eiffel Tower shimmer and sparkle. Most recently, my stepmother gamely ventured out to Marie Antoinette's former stomping grounds on a cold winter's day to help me with my research. When I moved there with Rick, Paris became not just a city I loved but my home. We shopped in the marchés, wrangled with the phone company, and wandered the city at all hours. Visiting friends—Nínive, Elizabeth, Sarah, Katie—all added further layers. Each of these people has deepened my knowledge and love of the city and helped me form an indelible attachment to it. I thank you all.

Another round of heartfelt thanks goes to those who helped me turn my abstract love of Paris into this very real book. To Pamela and Aubert de Villaine, for their unfailing generosity, kindness, and hospitality. To Emilie at Chronicle, for her patience and editorial wizardry. And again, to Rick, for keeping the home fires burning while I conducted research and for keeping his cool when I wrung my hands over looming deadlines.

I dedicate this book to Luc and Ben. I can't wait for you to discover your very own Paris someday soon.